"Steve Hayner has been first a hero and then a friend since I met him many years ago. He was a people magnet and an idea machine and an energy force. To follow the journey that he and Sharol traveled together through the valley of the shadow of death was a privilege and a heartbreak and an education in hope. I'm grateful their searing, aching, honest, inspiring words are now permanently available. I cannot imagine a human being who would not benefit from it."

John Ortberg, senior pastor of Menlo Park Presbyterian Church, author of *Soul Keeping*

"Seldom have I been as moved as in reading these epistles from Steve and Sharol Hayner—each ending 'Joyfully yours.' Through his life Steve helped so many to find life in all its fullness in Christ. Now, with his beloved Sharol, he guides us through the ending of life in fullness of hope. Thanks to InterVarsity Press for what I believe will become a classic."

Leighton Ford, author of *The Attentive Life*

"Few teach us how to die. Steve Hayner did. His honest, thoughtful, realistic reflections—full of faith and joy—are a gift to those of us who wonder what our final transition from life to 'life in the full' will be like. Steve and Sharol Hayner are the real deal—joyful followers of Jesus sharing how they together faced death."

Jeanette Yep, pastor, global and regional outreach, Grace Chapel, Lexington, MA

"'In life and in death we belong to God' are words often spoken by people of faith facing extraordinary life challenges. It was not until I witnessed those words made flesh in Steve and Sharol Hayner's exquisitely expressed reflections on their journey that I truly understood the depth of their meaning. Many books try to capture the essence of how to live while dying. *Joy in the Journey* hits the mark, leaving its readers certain of one thing: life lived joyfully is a gift that keeps on giving. Thank you, Steve!"

Deb Mullen, dean of faculty and executive vice president, Columbia Theological Seminary

"*Joy in the Journey* is a simple and yet profound testimony of a man of faith embracing life in death, and of a woman keeping faith and loving her husband all the way to the grave. It is a moving testimony of how it is that in the season of dying one comes to terms with what life is all about, the truths of the Gospel and God's call *today*. It is amazing how it all becomes clearer in the darker seasons of life. In these pages we receive glimpses into that 'over all presence of God' that makes gratitude and joy possible all the time, even in suffering, grieving and dying!"

David Zac Niringiye, PhD fellow, Religion, Culture and Public Life Project, Uganda Christian University Mukono

"This incredible little book offers a window into the soul of a dying man and his wife. Both of them are highly trained in theology, and some of their observations grapple courageously with God in the voice of the Psalmists. But most of their writings are a response to be faithful to God in the midst of this great interruption of their lives. Anyone who knew Steve will not be surprised that the response is always about joy."

Craig Barnes, president, Princeton Theological Seminary

"With remarkable candor, Steve and Sharol Hayner teach us how to live in the face of dying. Over nine months of physical decline, they lay bare a wide range of emotions—faith and fear, grace and grief, poignancy and pain. The journey, though hellish at times, is punctuated by the Lord's presence, family love and proactive friends. Years ago, I followed Steve to InterVarsity. Someday, when my health fails, I will follow him to glory. When that happens, I want to emulate his journey of dignity, courage and joy."

Alec Hill, president, InterVarsity Christian Fellowship

JOY IN THE JOURNEY

Finding Abundance in the Shadow of Death

STEVE & SHAROL HAYNER

Forewords by
MARK LABBERTON & ALEX GEE

IVP Books
An imprint of InterVarsity Press
Downers Grove, Illinois

InterVarsity Press
P.O. Box 1400, Downers Grove, IL 60515-1426
ivpress.com
email@ivpress.com

InterVarsity Press® is the book-publishing division of InterVarsity Christian Fellowship/USA®, a movement of students and faculty active on campus at hundreds of universities, colleges and schools of nursing in the United States of America, and a member movement of the International Fellowship of Evangelical Students. For information about local and regional activities, visit intervarsity.org.

The posts by Steve and Sharol Hayner were first published on CaringBridge.org.

The posts by Emilie Wagner were first published on www.mybigjesus.com.

Cover design: Cindy Kiple
Interior design: Beth McGill
Images: Orange Path, Marco, Cazzulini. Private Collection / Bridgeman Images

ISBN 978-0-8308-4447-0 (print)
ISBN 978-0-8308-9966-1 (digital)

Printed in Canada ♾

green press INITIATIVE *As a member of the Green Press Initiative, InterVarsity Press is committed to protecting the environment and to the responsible use of natural resources. To learn more, visit greenpressinitiative.org.*

Library of Congress Cataloging-in-Publication Data
Hayner, Stephen A.
Joy in the journey : finding abundance in the shadow of death / Steve and Sharol Hayner ; forewords by Mark Labberton and Alex Gee.
pages cm
Includes bibliographical references and index.
ISBN 978-0-8308-4447-0 (cloth : alk. paper)
1. Hayner, Stephen A. 2. Pancreas—Cancer—Patients—Religious life. 3. Pancreas—Cancer—Treatment. 4. Death—Religious aspects—Christianity. I. Title.
BV4910.33.H39 2015
248.8'61969940092—dc23
[B]

2015012621

P *20 19 18 17 16 15 14 13 12 11 10 9 8 7 6 5 4 3 2 1*
Y *32 31 30 29 28 27 26 25 24 23 22 21 20 19 18 17 16 15*

For our children and grandchildren

who faithfully shared this journey with us.

Papa loved you so much

and was so proud of you.

Contents

Foreword

Joy for Life and Death

Mark Labberton

I **was eighteen** and Steve was twenty-three when we first met. He was home from graduate study in Semitics and Near Eastern studies at Harvard, having graduated from Whitman College a year before I arrived on campus. Christian faith for me had just become a new category of life a few months before this. Steve was a teacher for our campus fellowship January term, and for one week he taught through the book of Genesis. It was in every way an experience of being "in the beginning."

Since that time, Steve has been my primary bellwether over the past forty-three years. Our two lives have unfolded in an uncoordinated tandem: college ministries, pastoral ministries, Presbyterian ordination, British PhDs, parachurch leadership, seminary faculty positions and then leadership of our respective seminaries (Steve at Columbia Theological Seminary, and I at Fuller Theological Seminary). We shared passions, work and commitments, as well as interests and convictions.

But my friendship with Steve was not about shared circumstances but lifeblood. I can hardly think of a significant experience, relationship or decision over all these years that we didn't share. This was made even more amazing to us both in that over these forty-three years we only lived in the same place for less than two of them.

The combination of the depth and the range of Steve's friendship over time was so much a part of the treasure of our relationship. He was a polymath, and there seemed no limit to the range and diversity of topics or issues, emotions or ideas, experiences or relationships that we could share and explore.

His buoyancy and enthusiasm reminded me of Tigger, while his thoughtfulness and scholarship evoked Erasmus. Bounding enthusiasm and generous encouragement were his daily modes of engagement.

ROOM TO BREATHE

Steve gave us an exceptionally important taste of God's grace. It is partly captured for me in Psalm 31:6-8:

I hate all this silly religion,
but you, GOD, *I trust.*
I'm leaping and singing in the circle of your love;
you saw my pain,
you disarmed my tormentors,
You didn't leave me in their clutches
but gave me room to breathe. (The Message)

Steve Hayner helped those he touched find room to breathe. For those of us with emotional, intellectual or religious claustrophobia, this was what we needed most from our pastor, mentor, teacher and friend: help finding the broad and open place of God's grace in which we could deeply and truly breathe.

Five years older than me, just enough to be ahead as an elder brother, Steve never pressed me toward anything except this: finding my life and vocation, my freedom and joy, in following Jesus. This was the place to breathe, and it was Steve's great theme. It was both as simple and as comprehensive as that. As teacher, pastor, friend, example, encourager, mentor and confessor, he led me toward a more faithful life, toward daily breathing in and out the love and mercy of God.

He was a deep-hearted but light-handed mentor. No part of my life was untouched by Steve's influence, yet no part was ever coerced. He did not corral people as a leader or shepherd, but rather invited us into God's abundant faithfulness. Steve moved from being my personal Bible encyclopedia to being a fellow traveler in the long, unexpected journey of faith. His relentless willingness to pay attention, to stay engaged in friendship, conversation, spiritual reflection and personal growth—these were all key traits for the many whom he loved and served. Life was never too complicated, or too broken or too fearsome, for Steve to offer in Jesus' name the room to breathe in the grace of God more deeply.

All of this is what Steve brought to his various leadership roles. This had been apparent throughout his early life, but by the time he was ordained a Presbyterian pastor and serving at University Presbyterian Church in Seattle, it was plain to all. His role was associate pastor for university ministries, and within a short time a few dozen students had become several hundred and then nearly a thousand. It was a social and spiritual phenomenon to see hundreds of students, principally from the University of Washington, descend on UPC at ten o'clock every Tuesday night for a communion service. This was not a service with balloons, skits or magic tricks. Steve just pointed students to Jesus Christ in all aspects of life, and for many it was the very air they needed and the life they sought.

When Steve became vice president for student affairs at Seattle Pacific University, it was a surprising move to a more administrative role, but one he carried out with all the instincts and compassion of a pastor. It extended and enlarged his commitment to university students, now expressed from inside a Christian university. It was always at center about the people, and he relentlessly pursued that purpose during his SPU years. He offered more broad space for more people—administrators, faculty, staff and students alike.

InterVarsity Christian Fellowship had been passing through a very difficult season of leadership transition when Steve was tapped to become the next president. It was a wounded, divided, anxious movement and needed a leader of courage, transparency, community and trust. Steve was that. It was a challenging period in which Steve's gracious, nonanxious presence, teaching, accessibility and love gradually made a significant difference. By the time that thirteen-year season in Madison, Wisconsin, was over, InterVarsity Christian Fellowship was in a far healthier place and on a trajectory toward ever deeper transformation. This has been especially evident in its commitment to multiethnic ministries, the discovery of that broad place of grace in which men and women of every ethnicity get to live and breathe the grace of God in light of, and not despite, their backgrounds and lives.

When Steve felt his time at IVCF was at an end, he stepped into a short two-year season of transition as an associate pastor at both High Point Community Church and Fountain of Life Covenant Church, both in Madison. Both were wonderful pastoral settings. The multiethnic themes and practices that had become so important during Steve's days with IVCF only continued and deepened through his friendship and partnership with Alex Gee at Fountain of Life.

All along, Steve had been committed to and involved with theological education. In his many years as an adjunct professor and board member for Fuller Theological Seminary, he contributed academic knowledge, pastoral insight and global vision. Taken all together, this is what made his move to Columbia Theological Seminary seem so natural for him. It could only be imagined that from Columbia's point of view, the hiring of the former president of IVCF may not have seemed natural or obvious. But from the start, Steve loved the faculty, the leadership, the board and the students of Columbia. With enthusiasm he sought to learn what he did not know, he savored those he met, he plunged into new courses. When he became president, it seemed like yet another unsought recognition of his gifts and abilities, and the joy he felt over the talent and diversity of people who became part of Columbia during these recent years (in significant partnership with Deb Mullen) was deeply gratifying to him and a source of great joy for Steve, and for Sharol as well.

During these same years he continued his contributions to World Vision, where he served on the board and felt with passion the need to care for the poor, especially children. Meanwhile, Steve was also serving as board member and chair for International Justice Mission. He did so in a fervent and passionate way, articulately leading the IJM board for a ministry making a singular response to those who are victims of violent oppression in places all around the world. This was a compelling mission, and Steve's facilitation of the board used his gifts and extended his heart that much further. He did it seamlessly and thoughtfully.

He wanted others served by World Vision and by IJM to have the room to breathe fully human lives, made in the image of God.

ADVANCED COURSEWORK IN JOY

For Steve, joy is that wide place of God's grace—that sees the world in great need, rescues us when we are caught, even caught by death, and invites us in all times and places to live in the place of grace where we can breathe. This explains why *joy* was the primary word in Steve's life. God's love is never scarce. God's capacity to meet us in our pain or sorrow, our confusion or sin, is best seen and experienced when we seek the One whose love is "abundantly far more than all we can ask or imagine" (Ephesians 3:20). Joy is life set in that reality. Nothing is excluded—including suffering and even death—and all is being remade.

Steve was an embodiment of an extravagant grace, grace within and beyond him. This was evident from when I first met him in my freshman dorm until I sat by his deathbed. He had great capacities intellectually and emotionally, organizationally and administratively. These would be goals for many, but for Steve they were incidental to the call to be with and for people.

Since his terminal diagnosis of pancreatic cancer during Easter week 2014, Steve's last nine months were like an advanced course in living and dying in faith, a story of honesty and hope. As he said, he had been training for this season his whole life, so perhaps it is no wonder that Steve did so well in the class! He would say it was simply a story of God's grace.

In the New Testament witness to the resurrection, it has always been fascinating to me that the principal evidence and meaning is borne in the stories of people who encounter the risen Christ.

Our Lord is risen, and it shows in the lives and witness of the women at the empty tomb. Peter is changed by his encounter with Jesus, who asks probing questions and offers healing assurance following the cross and resurrection. Despondent disciples on the road to Emmaus meet Jesus in the breaking of the bread and recognize him in their burning hearts. Paul, who was bent on stopping the whole Jesus project, is stopped in his tracks and given a new life. Those touched by the resurrection of Jesus can breathe anew and afresh of a life beyond themselves, or their failings or sin, or their suffering and loss—beyond even death.

In Jesus' name, Steve gave us room to breathe. He gave us joy in the midst of wrestling and questioning and seeking and hurting and hoping because he was living a resurrection life. He was not a nervous Christian. His only comfort in life and in death was that he belonged body and soul, in life and in death, not to himself, but to his faithful Savior, Jesus Christ.

His—and Sharol's—profound witness to us all in these last months, and captured in what will follow here, was not a tale of people straining to find an absent God, but of lives largely free of entitlement or presumption, of people with grateful hearts filled by God's resurrection life and set free for the honest adventure of hearing and following the call to follow Jesus and, in the midst of all else, to find life even in death.

The hope of the resurrection was Steve's life. It is the broad space to breathe in life and in death; it is the place to love and affirm, to encourage and to persevere; it is the place to take up our cross for the joy set before us. It is this living, breathing life that holds all human sorrows and injustices and alone will make all things right. Steve's resurrected life was just in line with the New Testament witnesses.

It was the day before he died—Steve was in a revived state of full awareness and presence after a couple of days of seeming to have nearly left us—when in humor and tears and great love some of us gathered around his bed for a small Communion service.

Steve was back: fully conversational, emotionally engaged and physically weak but functional. We prayed, we shared the cup and the bread, we sang and we cried, and then Steve, the one dying and yet fully alive, pronounced the benediction one more time over our grieving, loving, joyful circle. From the deathbed of the dying man came the words and voice of hope and resurrection over all of us: "Now to the One who is able to do exceedingly abundantly beyond all we could ask or even imagine according to his power at work in us, to God be the glory in the church and in Christ Jesus both now and forever more. Amen" (Ephesians 3:20-21, paraphrase).

Steve Hayner's resurrected life, lived in ordinary and exceptional days, is what drew us to him and to the audience of One before whom he called all of us to seek and to find our lives too—in our living, in our dying and in our living again.

Breathe deeply the love and mercy, truth and justice of Jesus Christ, for this is the broad place where we find the God of joy for life and even for death.

Foreword

Greatness That Comes from Service

Alex Gee

Death challenges us. It challenges what we believe about life. It challenges what we believe about death. It challenges what we believe about faith. And it raises questions of how what we believe stays with us once a loved one has crossed over.

As Steve's friend, I want to be careful not to make him seem bigger than life. He was not perfect, but he was great because he served. I learned so much from Steve about my strengths and my gifts, servant leadership and trust. I am a better man because of my accountability to him and his affection for me. I once asked Steve why he spent so much time with me. He told me that an old mentor once taught him that every young man needs an older man who thinks he is great.

Steve knew how my issues of fatherlessness would often creep up on me. The only way I had planned to get over it was to become a dad. But for years this eluded me as we lost two daughters to premature birth. Then on Thanksgiving morning during my wife's third pregnancy, her water broke. I know how hospitable the Hayners are on holidays and how much they need family time, but I needed an older man who was a pastor. I called my mother, my mother-in-law and Steve. He came to the hospital that morning.

He was too Presbyterian to speak in the way of my black Pentecostal tradition, "Thus saith the Lord," but he spoke to me with certainty in the cafeteria that day. He looked at me and said, "She is going to be small, but you are going to bring this one home." And he was right.

Many people remember that I spoke at Urbana '96 and showed a picture of my daughter, Lexi, when she was only three weeks old. But what people don't realize is that that was really Steve's speaking slot as the president of InterVarsity. He asked me to share that time with him because he felt I had a voice that needed to be exposed to broader white evangelicalism. Steve shared power, and he positioned me in ways I never imagined.

After he left InterVarsity, I talked Steve into being my associate pastor. People couldn't believe that I would ask the former president of InterVarsity to serve as my associate pastor. What a coup! But we were friends, and I could do that. First I said, "I need you to preach sometime." Our church was predominantly black at the time, and Steve said, "Oh no, no. I can't do that. What would I say? I'm from Walla Walla." I said, "Steve, if you don't do this, then you don't value what I have to do every time I step into your world. You need to do this to understand me and to understand what it costs and what it takes." And he did it.

One day when I was out of town, Steve led a Bible study for leaders in our church who called me later and said, "We really like your friend."

I asked, "Was it his exegesis of Jeremiah? Was it the way he opened Scripture? Was it the Ephesians thing?"

"No, no," they said, "that was tight and all."

"So what did he do?"

They replied, "He got up and said, 'I don't know what I'm

doing in this multicultural church with my little white [bleep].'" He was automatically in.

My very last conversation with Steve was as he was transitioning. He sent me a text message saying, "I will probably be leaving today." I thought, *Oh, my God. Who sends a text message to their friends saying I'm out of here?* Later we did have a phone conversation. I got to say that he had been the most consistent and caring older male figure in my life and that I loved him for that. He was a great man because he served the least among us until we didn't feel like the least anymore. One of the things that people loved most about Steve was who we were when we were around him.

After walking with Steve in his final months, I am considering where his life challenges mine. Where is God calling me to invest my time and energy? I'm asking what and who I need in life in order to face death with hope, joy and confidence. What changes do I need to make today in order to finish well? As you journey with Steve and Sharol in the following pages, how will you answer these questions?

Preface

Sharol

What follows is a journey of two people who never imagined that in their sixties they would face what they thought would be reserved for their eighties or nineties.

Of course, this is not the beginning of our journey. Forty-five years ago Steve and I met in Boston, fell in love and decided that as a couple we would follow Jesus wherever he might lead. We traveled well together. One friend has said that in his mind, Steve and Sharol is a hyphenated name. We weren't simply partners but were yoked together as one. And it was true, at least in the many ways that God allowed us to serve together. But we were also individuals, similar in many ways but very different in others. It is that togetherness and those differences that we brought with us on Steve's cancer journey, which began on Easter weekend 2014.

The entries from the CaringBridge website were never intended as a book—only as a means of communicating with family and friends around the world. The response has been overwhelming. We are as surprised as the boy who gave Jesus his lunch of five loaves and two fish. Jesus took that simple lunch, blessed it and then fed thousands of hungry people who had gathered around him. My prayer is that thousands more will be fed by what we have simply offered to Jesus and now to you.

HEALTH UPDATE: During Easter weekend I began to feel out of sorts and experienced some unusual symptoms. On Monday morning, April 21, I went to the doctor, who did tests and made a preliminary diagnosis that I was having gall bladder issues. He sent me for an ultrasound, which turned out to be negative for gallstones, and then a CT scan, which revealed a small mass on the head of my pancreas. On Wednesday I was able to get in to see a wonderful surgeon at Emory who was 95 percent certain that I had a malignant tumor. Because of the location, the tumor was blocking the bile duct and causing me to become jaundiced, but it is also operable. We decided I would have a Whipple procedure, which is a complex but effective surgery. That surgery is now scheduled for Tuesday, May 6.

WAITING

Now that it is May, the surgery day feels a lot closer at hand. I don't feel very well. The jaundice makes me tired, and I have a variety of abdominal pains. I also look like I've been using a bad bronzing product—just a little too yellow to be attractive. The hardest part is that I have no appetite, can't eat animal fats, and am continuing to lose weight. I'm lighter now than at any time since I was in junior high.

The doctors and hospital staff at Emory could not be more helpful. From the "Patient's Surgery Guide" to the pre-op physical and "fast-track" admissions process, all has gone very smoothly indeed.

We have been overwhelmed by the number of people who

have written emails, cards and letters indicating that they are praying. It is humbling, and it brings great joy.

We continue to take one day at a time. I'm not really worried. Over the years I have done what I can to take care of my health, and I am actually in exceptional health for a sixty-five-year-old. So now by God's grace I enter the next chapter of the journey over which I have very little control. Medically I'm in great hands. *And God is good!*

Steve *May 2*

HEALTH UPDATE: Today I was scheduled for a small biopsy, which my surgeon really wants before the surgery itself. We got to Emory Hospital and were all ready to go. But unfortunately, as sometimes happens, another very complex surgery was occupying the operating room with the MRI, and it lasted several hours longer than expected. So, my biopsy is now rescheduled for Tuesday—and my surgical date will be postponed too.

GOD'S TIME

Sharol and I continue to be relaxed.

We're on God's timetable in this—clearly not ours. We continue to be carried along and sustained by the Spirit and the love and prayers of our amazing friends.

Steve *May 7*

HEALTH UPDATE: Yesterday I had a pre-op biopsy because my doctor saw a couple of very small lesions (4 mm) on my liver in an MRI. As it turns out, these are also cancer, which means that the surgery is now "off the table" as an option. We now will move toward what I am calling medical plan B. Tomorrow I will have an ERCP along with the insertion of a bile duct stent so that my digestive system can get working again. After that we will decide on the chemotherapy protocol that will be used to treat the cancer.

PLAN B

Honestly, the hardest part of this is not the seeming setback, but rather the delay in starting some sort of treatment that will begin to relieve the increasing symptoms of the jaundice. My energy is very low. I continue to lose weight. And I just plain feel sick most of the time.

I'm sorry that I cannot respond to each of the incredible cards, emails and texts that continue to pour in. We feel so loved.

Sharol *May 7*

FIERY FURNACE

Hopefully this procedure tomorrow will bring back some quality of life before we consider next steps.

Thank you for the many prayers and expressions of love. We are overwhelmed, humbled and thankful.

We are definitely in the fiery furnace from Daniel 3, but we are not alone. God's presence is very evident.

Steve *May 8*

THE WAY OF TRUST

We returned a little while ago from my latest procedure (ERCP). Hopefully this will take care of the jaundice and people won't call me "Sunshine" anymore. I've been wearing a lot of yellow recently so as not to call attention to my current skin tone.

So now we will wait a few days to see if my appetite comes back and I can begin to gain back a few pounds and a little strength. The next stage will be a meeting with the medical oncologist to begin discussing treatment options. Reading about metastatic pancreatic cancer can be pretty scary, but we continue to be calm and are taking one day at a time.

There are never any guarantees in this life, and this is a chance to take Jesus' words to heart: "And can any of you by worrying add a single hour to your span of life?" (Matthew 6:27).

We'll choose the way of trust and joy instead.

Steve *May 12*

HEALTH UPDATE: I have lost fifteen pounds in the last three weeks. I'm mostly in the mode of trying to manage symptoms, trying to eat when I can and trying to gain back a little weight.

WARRIOR

Several decades ago in Seattle, we sang a wonderful song called "Victorious Warrior," based on Zephaniah 3:17:

The LORD *your God is in*
your midst,
A victorious warrior.
He will exult over you with
joy,
He will be quiet in His love,
He will rejoice over you with
shouts of joy. (NASB)

For some reason, this little chorus has been running through my head for the last several days and has served as an encouragement to me.

We are incredibly grateful for the prayers and well wishes of so many friends from the various circles and timelines of our lives. Every day I feel the privilege of it all.

This just sucks. . . . I hate this ordeal for you. I'm stomping my feet and wish with all my heart that you weren't having to experience any of this and could just have kept on doing the fabulous things you were doing without jaundice and medical procedures. I've shared these thoughts with the Great Physician in whose loving hands your care is kept so your Medical Staff is well-informed. . . . My prayers join the chorus of prayers confidently lifting you up to heaven's mercy and healing. . . . Let the love and prayers wash over you and bear you up. I give thanks to God that you have been and are God's agents in bringing community into being.

SUE WESTALL

Sharol *May 13*

HEALTH UPDATE: On May 14 Steve and I will meet for the first time with the oncologist at Emory to talk about next steps in Steve's treatment as well as how to control some of the cancer symptoms he is experiencing. We are eager to take this next step and figure out what might be ahead for us in the coming weeks and months.

CARRIED

We continue to be carried through this somewhat surreal experience. Mostly I am in awe and very thankful for the gifts of friendship and encouragement.

I've always had music in my head, and it is now there more than ever. Today I'm singing over and over in my mind a song called "Still" by Hillsong: "Find rest my soul in Christ alone."

Steve has good days and bad days, sometimes with enough energy to walk a block and sometimes not. Sometimes he can eat and sometimes not. Today is ending better than it began.

In the meantime, I'm trying to attend some of the many May programs and recitals of our granddaughters. It's good to remember what normal life feels like. And we anticipate a new grandson in Nashville in the next two weeks. Life goes on.

Paul's words in 2 Corinthians 1:9-11 come to mind often. Coming out of a desperate situation, he writes,

> Indeed, we felt that we had received the sentence of death so that we would rely not on ourselves but on God who raises the dead. He who rescued us from so deadly a peril will continue to rescue us; on him we have set our hope that he will rescue us again, as you also join in helping us by your prayers, so that many will give thanks on our behalf for the blessing granted us through the prayers of many.

May it be so.

Sharol *May 15*

HEALTH UPDATE: Steve will start a chemo protocol called Folfirinox on May 28. After a port is implanted next week, he will receive two of the meds every two weeks at the infusion center and then will wear a pump for forty-eight hours with the third drug. This is the most rigorous and potentially toxic regimen, but the doctor feels that Steve will do well with it.

OVERWHELMED

This all feels very overwhelming to me. I have to keep remembering:

- One step at a time.
- One day at a time.
- God will be faithful to hold us and carry us no matter what happens.

The level of change in our lives keeps rising, but again, I don't have to embrace it all at once. But I do wish there were an easier fix! "Not my will but yours be done" (Luke 22:42).

Steve *May 15*

HEALTH UPDATE: We spent almost four hours (including labs and waiting) with various members of the medical oncology team who are now joining the company of companions for the next phase of our journey. The team at Winship Cancer Institute at Emory is multifaceted and amazing—and they are obviously functioning well as a team.

CANCER AND CALLING

Today is the first full day of the next chapter in our journey.

We received loads of information, we had a chance to discuss not only the treatment options but also our goals and values, and we learned how we would be accessing all of the resources available as we take each step. Sharol and our friend Mary Banks Knechle (a trained parish nurse and patient advocate) listened, took notes and asked fabulous questions along the way. I worked to absorb as much information as possible.

Never once did I feel like just a project or a case.

In the end the day was enormously encouraging to me, and I came home feeling empowered. My response was quite different from Sharol's, but we both know that this will frequently be the case in this journey. While we share many of the same circumstances and values, we don't share the same internal or external challenges.

An important part of this period is learning to love each other the way each of us needs to be loved—and giving each other space to do the work we need to do individually.

The medical team will work with me to minimize the long list of potential side effects, though I expect that I will have some days ahead when I will have some real physical challenges.

What many want to know is the prognosis. Will this work? Can they cure this cancer? These are not my questions.

All life on planet earth is terminal, and while we can certainly contribute to our own well-being in amazing ways, none of us is ultimately in control. One day, my life will be swallowed up by Life. And for today, I am choosing truth, joy and love wherever and however I can.

I am resolute in my desire to learn, to fulfill my calling and to engage each day with as much joy as I am graciously given or can borrow.

I'm apprehensive about the unknown, and I am certainly feeling knocked around. But I am not afraid—at least yet.

To paraphrase Psalm 121, "I lift my eyes to the hills. Is that where my help comes from? No, my help comes from the Lord, who is maker of both heaven and earth—and who holds me in the palm of God's hand."

Sharol *May 16*

MY FEEBLE CRY

We are both feeling encouraged today. With Steve having more energy and feeling almost "normal" for a great portion of the day, I am beginning to gain hope for these next weeks. I honestly thought that Steve curled up on the bed with the TV on, hardly able to eat and wrestling with pain, would be the norm. Steve is managing the pain very well now, is able to eat and is much more cheery. I thank God for you all and for your prayers. We are being carried along by them.

This is my story for today from Psalm 40:1-3. God heard my feeble cry.

I waited patiently for the LORD*;*
he inclined to me and heard my cry.
He drew me up from the desolate pit,
out of the miry bog,
and set my feet upon a rock,
making my steps secure.

He put a new song in my mouth,
a song of praise to our God.
Many will see and fear,
and put their trust in the LORD.

Steve

May 18

HEALTH UPDATE: I'm thankful to report that the jaundice is now largely cleared. The last two days I've almost felt my "normal" self again. My energy is at about 85 percent (rather than 10 percent). My appetite is back (yesterday I ate three "regular" meals plus snacks).

GRACE LESSONS

I was able to attend Columbia Theological Seminary's graduation worship (sitting in the balcony), our granddaughters' dance recital and a faculty family picnic. Honestly it felt like something of a miracle after feeling so generally awful for a month. My pain is now being managed, so even that isn't bothersome.

Sharol and I have both handled the last few days quite differently. All of the information about what chemo could hold has given me encouragement because we have something of a game plan before us now—the outlines of a plan to be executed.

For Sharol it has been overwhelming.

The list of possible side effects related to the three chemotherapies that I will be administered is pretty daunting, even though the doctor has confidence that I will do well because of my overall good health and strength. Still the realities of the unknowns and the complexities have been swirling in Sharol's head.

So we're learning how to listen again to one another's heart. I can't "fix" this for Sharol (or myself). But we can hold each other with understanding and sensitivity.

We're both learning new lessons about grace. Grace can never be learned once and for all. It must be explored through each new circumstance. It must be experienced, received and savored. It defies scrutiny but requires reflection.

Two nights ago I was awake (I lost pain control for an hour or so) and while I prayed I realized that I had almost lost coherence and just found myself like a small child settling in to the comforting arms of a parent for a long and gentle embrace.

Your ongoing prayers and your kind words of encouragement and love bring hope and joy, not to mention distraction from some of the daily grind of this disease. And thank you for passing the word along. That's a help, too, since one of the small challenges of this time is how to suggest ways for folks to be helpful while needing to maintain some necessary time boundaries so that we aren't overwhelmed by "help." (That's such an ironic statement!)

Joyfully, Steve

Steve *May 20*

HEALTH UPDATE: The procedure to install the infusion port will be Friday morning. This is the last major piece of preparation (apart from my work at simply getting stronger and healthier) for chemotherapy, which begins on Wednesday, May 28.

SUNSHINE. FAMILY. FOOD.

I continue to feel good. The pain is under control. My appetite is good. We have family here visiting for a couple of days, and it's wonderful to be able to engage and to feel good along the way.

Today I will enjoy the sunshine, my family and the pleasure of eating.

The family. Photo by Hannah Hicks.

Steve *May 23*

HEALTH UPDATE: Today I had the chemo infusion port installed. It's a little "permanent" IV port under the skin right below my collar bone on the right side. The advantage of this is that I will not have to have an IV installed every time I need an infusion or other procedure where they have to take blood. We know the routines now for these sorts of things. The teams at Emory are super and make it very comfortable and relatively efficient for patients—although there is still a lot of waiting as with any medical procedures.

I've been praying Psalm 23 for you these days: "Yea, though I walk through the valley of the shadow of death, I will fear no evil: for thou art with me; thy rod and thy staff they comfort me" (KJV). Just have this clear and overwhelming sense that God's Spirit will be hovering over you these days as he was in the beginning, that you both are covered completely in his loving care.

LINDA BREEDEN

FRIENDSHIP

I continue to enjoy the beautiful days, the relatively healthy experience (little pain, good appetite, reasonable energy) and the preparations for chemo, which begins next Wednesday. We'll know a lot more about what life will be like in the next couple of months after this first experience.

Steve fifteen pounds lighter

Thank you for your prayers and for your wonderful expressions of love and friendship. I will never take this sort of thing for granted again.

Steve

May 26

NEW LIFE

Last evening our fifth grandchild, Jack William Hayner (10 pounds, 4 ounces), was born. His parents, Chip and Kristen Hayner (in Nashville), and sister, Lainey (3), are all doing well.

"Looks like he can carry his mom home!" (a comment by Mary Hoffman on Facebook).

We are all rejoicing.

> *On your journey through this chapter in life, please know that your ministry is not compromised. Your ministry is continuing and is expanding. . . . Each and every day you are teaching all of us what it truly means to place our trust, hope and faith in Jesus Christ—even during times of great trials. May you feel God's constant presence and his steadfast love, as you stand firmly—experiencing his peace and joy.*
>
> MARTHA THOMPSON WAGNER

Steve

May 27

THE DAY BEFORE CHEMO

In J. B. Phillips's translation of the New Testament, he renders Romans 5:1-5 this way:

> Since then it is by faith that we are justified, let us grasp the fact that we have peace with God through our Lord Jesus Christ. Through [Christ] we have confidently entered into this new relationship of grace, and here we take our stand, in happy certainty of the glorious things he has for us in the future.

> This doesn't mean, of course, that we have only a hope of future joys—we can be full of joy here and now even in our trials and troubles. Taken in the right spirit these very things will give us patient endurance; this in turn will develop a mature character, and a character of this sort produces a steady hope, a hope that will never disappoint us. Already we have some experience of the love of God flooding through our hearts by the Holy Spirit given to us.

These were great verses to wake up to this morning. Life is lived in the grace of Jesus through and through—whether the grace is obvious in our immediate circumstances or not. With Jesus at work in our lives, God's "good" is always being done and we always continue to grow and to be transformed.

I realized this morning that the next chapter of this journey is the scariest part for me so far. It's easier for me to think about dying than it is to think about feeling sick all the time—or having the quality of my life and ministry thoroughly compromised. And there are so many unknowns that come with chemotherapy.

"Full of joy here and now even in our trials and troubles." That's where I want to stand.

Sharol *May 27*

ON THE EVE OF CHEMO

As I think back on the past two weeks since we've known Steve was headed into this treatment, the one word that describes my interior life is *quiet*.

I've experienced amazing peace and the ability to take one day at a time. I've felt sheltered (even hindered) from looking ahead and have had a profound sense of the importance of each day. This could only be a gift from God—that surpassing-human-understanding kind of peace described in Philippians 4.

In the midst of the quiet, I've thought about so many things.

I've pondered the ways we talk about hope. We hope for this and for that as if the fulfillment of our hopes will be a positive outcome or the measure of our contentment or success.

I've wondered what to hope for.

Complete healing?

Long life?

A few more months or years?

But I'm newly aware of the many places in Scripture, especially in the Psalms, where hope is centered in God alone. God is the one secure place for my hope because it's not dependent on my changing circumstances. God is so much bigger and more powerful than my circumstances. How very freeing.

I've thought about the story of the paralyzed man whose friends carried him to Jesus to be healed in Mark 2:2-5:

> So many gathered around that there was no longer room for them, not even in front of the door; and he was speaking the word to them. Then some people came, bringing to him a paralyzed man, carried by four of them. And when they could not bring him to Jesus because of the crowd, they removed the roof above him; and after having dug through it, they let down the mat on which the paralytic lay. When Jesus saw their faith, he said to the paralytic, "Son, your sins are forgiven."

You all are the friends who are carrying Steve to Jesus to be healed, and I've wanted to be part of that faithful crowd. But in sometimes finding it hard to know how to pray, I've recognized that it's okay to crawl onto the stretcher with Steve and be carried myself. That too is so freeing. (Both Steve and I have actually felt freed up to pray for many of you.)

Having just been to Nashville for twenty-four hours to welcome our new grandson, Jack, and love on Lainey, Chip and Kristen, I reflected on Psalm 131 during my drive home today. It is a psalm of quietness and contentment.

But I have calmed and quieted my soul,
like a weaned child with its mother.

I've witnessed the frantic cries of a baby longing for his mother's breast. The weaned child has learned to trust that her mother will provide for her. I'm convinced that God has been and will continue to provide for us. I don't have to worry or wonder. This is also freeing.

Know that we are so grateful for each of you and count it a privilege to have your companionship on this journey. Here we go.

Sharol *May 28*

HEALTH UPDATE: Thankfully, we were admitted early to Steve's chemotherapy bay in Emory's Infusion Center, where Steve was first administered the necessary antinausea meds followed by two of the three drugs that make up this particular protocol called Folfirinox. We are so impressed with the staff at Emory and with our oncology nurse in particular. Steve felt quite normal during the whole process except during the second drug when some hives started to pop up (which is rather common for Steve, who has numerous allergies). The nurse took Steve off the chemo and gave him Benadryl. He was able to finish the second drug without problems so that we got home around 5:00 p.m. He is now wearing a fanny pack with a pump and the third drug, which is being infused into his system for the next forty-six hours.

WE MADE IT!

You would think we had just finished a marathon, when in truth we have just run the first leg of a very long race. But we made it thanks to your prayers and God's grace. Though it was a very long day, it was a good day from start to finish.

Steve is feeling very tired (thanks to the Benadryl) and fatigued (thanks to the chemo drugs), but otherwise none the worse for wear, for which we are so grateful. We believe that your prayers have made a big difference in our day. Other side effects may show up in the next few days, but we are praying that these will be minimal and manageable. Thankfully, there are antidotes for every symptom. As you can imagine, Steve is very organized and has a spreadsheet that tells him what to take when and then keeps track of when he takes each med.

We are feeling loved, encouraged, strengthened and so very grateful tonight.

But this I call to mind,
and therefore I have hope:
The steadfast love of the Lord *never ceases,*
his mercies never come to an end;
they are new every morning;
great is your faithfulness.

"The Lord *is my portion," says my soul,*
"therefore I will hope in him." (Lamentations 3:21-24)

Sharol *May 29*

HEALTH UPDATE: Steve's day started out with some nausea, but by noon he was able to eat a small lunch. But this afternoon, the nausea really set in and it's been difficult for Steve to get on top of it. Thankfully, we go in tomorrow at two o'clock when the pump will be removed, and we can talk with the nurse in the infusion center about how better to deal with these symptoms.

ROUGH DAY

It's been a teary day for me between saying goodbye to a dear friend who is moving, and watching Steve suffer. I'm thankful that I know in my head and have experienced before that God is "a very present help in trouble" (Psalm 46:1). Grateful too that when I don't know how to pray, Jesus is interceding for Steve. And I also know that God hears your prayers. It's time to lean into those truths.

My admiration for those of you who have walked this way before us has skyrocketed today. You are my heroes. I'm grateful that we're not alone and that we can ask you to pray for some relief tonight. We need you in the valleys as well as on the heights. I also am learning that I need to develop new muscles and new stamina for this journey. Thanks for helping to hold us up.

A NEW MORNING

Twenty-five years ago when we first moved to Madison, Wisconsin, on a particularly gray morning when all was covered with snow, in loneliness I prayed that God would somehow let me know his presence. As I stood at my kitchen window, I saw on a limb, silhouetted against the white snow, a brilliant red cardinal. I thought, *God is indeed present!* Ever since then when I see a cardinal, I am reminded that the Lord is near.

Our grandchildren love cardinals because Grammie loves them. Last week, Emilie's children, Claire (7), Anna (5) and David (2), painted little cardinals and hid them all over our house. I have been discovering them all week, but this morning they stood out as a huge reminder that God is indeed present among us.

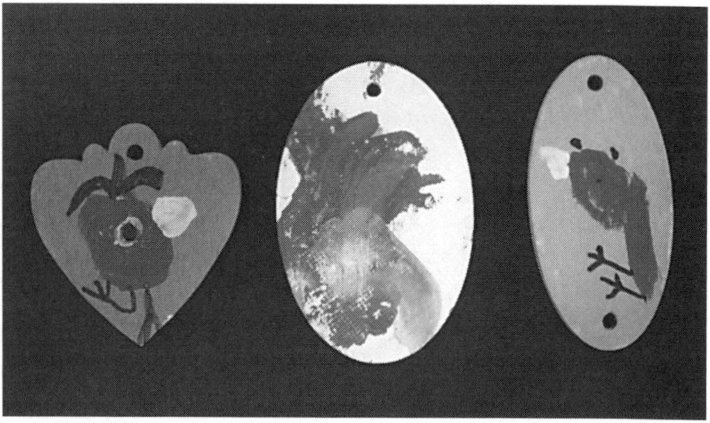

Cardinals painted by the grandchildren

Steve and I both slept well last night. He ate a bowl of oatmeal this morning and is now napping. It's a new morning—full of God's mercies.

May you see cardinals all through your day.

The Lord is near.

Steve *June 1*

SPACE FOR QUESTIONS

I haven't written since the days I began my chemotherapy because I just haven't had the energy to do so. They have been days full of sheer exhaustion, nausea that has come and gone like great waves, and trying to understand many of the other unusual symptoms that my body is experiencing right now.

Today I woke up feeling so much better. I actually got out of bed, took a shower, shaved and went down to a nice breakfast of French toast. It was probably a bit much, but it was nice to taste something that was good. I have been fastidious today with taking the right meds at the correct times (I am on seven), and that has seemingly paid off too. I did come down with hives again today and had to add some Benadryl to the whole routine, but that's a small price to pay.

I am reading a little book by Parker Palmer right now, titled *A Hidden Wholeness*. He writes about the process of one person talking with another about the deepest questions of their heart.

> When you speak to me about your deepest questions, you do not want to be fixed or saved: you want to be seen and heard, to have your truth acknowledged and honored. If your problem is soul-deep, your soul alone knows what

> you need to do about it, and my presumptuous advice will only drive your soul back into the woods. So the best service I can render when you speak to me about such a struggle is to hold you faithfully in a space where you can listen to your inner teacher.

I find this so true right now. Various questions move through my mind—some impatient for answers, and many others as if they are simply aware that their very presence creates a challenge or a stumbling place within a landscape on which my current life is being revealed, understood, remodeled and remade. Those who have joined me in the process have done best when they have just stood by—or perhaps shined a little new light into a hence unknown corner.

Sharol

June 4

RELEARNING TRUST

When I was a little girl, my family was part of a church in California where at the Sunday evening service we would sing several of the old favorite gospel hymns. While I have forgotten many of them, several have stuck with me through the years. "Simply Trusting Every Day" is one of those songs that has stuck.

Simply trusting every day;
Trusting through a stormy way;
Even when my faith is small,
Trusting Jesus, that is all.

Trusting as the moments fly,
Trusting as the days go by,

Trusting Him, whate'er befall,
Trusting Jesus, that is all.

Singing if my way be clear,
Praying if the path be drear;
If in danger, for Him call,
Trusting Jesus, that is all.

Trusting as the moments fly,
Trusting as the days go by,
Trusting Him, whate'er befall,
Trusting Jesus, that is all.

This is a time when we are learning to trust Jesus every day. Each day is different. Yesterday was a difficult day for Steve when he couldn't get on top of his nausea. Today he was able to eat seminormally and to attend a meeting with board members from Columbia Seminary. But tonight, he is struggling with pain and nausea.

It's a tough journey.

Please pray that we would be wise, hopeful, trusting and patient. We believe in a trustworthy God who fully knows us, perfectly loves us and hears our cries.

The LORD *is my strength and my shield;*
in him my heart trusts;
so I am helped, and my heart exults,
and with my song I give thanks to him. (Psalm 28:7)

BULLET-POINT DAYS

Today is the first day in many when I have had the energy to think about writing. I tried a bit yesterday, but the notorious "chemo brain" was making it almost impossible to type without having to correct every other word. These are the parts of the journey where I just have to think about slogging along.

Some days have been really discouraging with higher nausea and very low energy, and using almost all my capacity just to sort out how to manage the various medications that are prescribed "as needed" to deal with some of the side effects of the chemo—and then the side effects of the side effects. These are what I am coming to describe as "bullet-point days"—days when the best that I can do is to live into the bullet-point aphorisms that have often marked my life:

- One day at a time.
- It's a long obedience in the same direction.
- Patience really is about patience—and I've always been way too prone to hurry.
- Lean in and rest. Let striving cease. Resting is not the opposite of productivity.

I have thought about how often I have advised people to let others carry them in their faith during these times—like the four friends in the story about Jesus in Mark 2:1-12. It was not the paralytic's faith to which Jesus responded initially, but the simple faith of the man's friends.

I woke up one day this week and realized that I couldn't

locate anything like a genuine "faith" inside me that would provide enough strength to pray or to reflect or to meditate. But then it occurred to me that I didn't need any. God's grace is not about me. So whatever God has for me is going to come from outside anyway.

There are so many people who have asked us how they can help—and that morning I realized that they were helping by simply "being faith" for me. They were welcoming God's grace when I couldn't even do that much.

And so, I nestled into my pillow and enjoyed a moment of realization that I was simply being held by joy.

Steve *June 10*

HEALTH UPDATE: My day tomorrow will consist of bloodwork at the crack of dawn—then a meeting with the medical oncology team to make sure that all my numbers are as they should be before we call in the big cannons. Hopefully by 8:30 a.m. I will be comfortably situated in the "infusion room" at the Cancer Institute, where they will prepare all the pharmaceuticals and begin the slow (five- to six-hour) process of infusing them one by one through the nifty "infusion port" in my chest.

EVERYTHING WHICH IS YES

It's hard to imagine that I could actually be looking forward to the next round of chemo, which begins early tomorrow morning. Six days ago I was still feeling so sick that I couldn't imagine how anyone could agree to do this more than once, knowing that you are bombarding your body with chemicals that are killing off (hopefully) the bad rather indiscriminately with the good.

But a few days make a big change in perspective. Since last Friday I have felt better and stronger every day. I am sorting out better ways to manage my arsenal of medications, and I have enjoyed the luxury of food tasting good again.

I'm ready to go for the next round. This time may be quite different from the last—even much more difficult. But it will be good to have more than one data point behind me. Sharol will likely keep you up to speed in the next few days. I doubt that I will have the strength.

What has continued to invade my mind today is an e.e. cummings life-affirming celebration of what it means to be alive and aware today. The poem is called "i thank You God for most this amazing."

Sharol *June 11*

HEALTH UPDATE: Here are some comments from Steve: "The day in the infusion bay today went well—not as long as expected and with very few immediate side effects. The doctor this morning was encouraged, too, by the strength of my 'numbers' (mostly the blood tests, which remain strong, and the fall of the bilirubin count, where normal is 0.3-1.2 and mine was as high as 16.7 two weeks ago—and today was 0.9). So now I'm home on 'the pump' for the next two days. These were the really hard days the last time, especially with nausea, lethargy and exhaustion. So as you pray, please pray for healing and protection."

DAYS OF HOPE

While we know what the next days might hold, we are facing them with hope. The doctor is adding some meds that potentially will lessen the nausea. And so far, Steve is feeling strong and was able to eat a healthy dinner tonight along with a piece and a half of pound cake. We do, however, count on your prayers even as we thank God for the many gifts of this day, including each of you.

Steve *June 12*

HEALTH UPDATE: This evening I was comparing my personal journal for the second day of my first chemo treatment (May 29) with what happened today. Two weeks ago I could hardly write even for myself because of the nausea, the pain and other side effects that I was trying to deal with. I think that my big mistake was misinterpreting the doctor's instructions to take something "as needed"—what he really meant to say was, "Take this because you're going to need it." Waiting for certain symptoms to show up was often too late. So I've been on a careful medication regimen today and it has helped immensely.

ALLOWING GRACE TO FLOW

While the day has still been no picnic—as I listen even now to the little whir of my chemo pump continuing to infuse the drugs for another eighteen hours or so—I have felt much, much better than I did during the first round of chemo. I have had virtually no nausea, no pain (except with the occasional hiccup and belching marathons, which are an interesting side effect), and my appetite has stayed good. I have been able to eat three healthy meals as well as the requisite snacks, and enjoy the company of a few of the family members who have stopped by. So thanksgiving abounds!

I also began today with almost an hour of centering meditation, including quiet music and focus on allowing the healing energy of the Spirit and the chemo to do its work.

I've learned so much in the last three years as an "activist" by nature of the importance of such ancient biblical practices as quiet, gratitude, attentiveness and slow, deep breathing—all of which help to bring my physical body into greater alignment with the emotional, mental, social and spiritual parts of my life, and allow God's grace and love to flow more abundantly.

Your thoughts, prayers and love today have clothed me once again in joy.

Steve *June 18*

HEALTH UPDATE: I was hoping to report about all that we have learned during this second chemo application that has helped us with managing the side effects. And indeed, there are a number of things that we have learned. But overall I would say that this experience has been more difficult than the first. I suppose that this is not to be unexpected since the whole point is to give the cancer a one-two (and eventually more) punch. But I have to remember that giving the cancer a solid punch also means giving some of the otherwise healthy systems in my body a punch too.

THE GIFT OF BEING REMEMBERED

Today it has been a whole week since the last chemo began—and the first day that I can say I am feeling a little more upbeat. Especially this week, the nausea has been harder to deal with and I have felt generally drained and exhausted. I have slept more than the previous time. But this was the day that things turned around the last time, and we're hoping that it will be the same this time as well.

We have several dear friends and family who are coming for a visit this weekend. We're both looking forward to that. There won't be any great pressure on us, which is good, and I will have the opportunity to just disappear if I need to get some rest. I certainly don't mind being the "excuse" for a little reunion so long as I don't have a lot of responsibility in helping people to have a good time. And let's face it, I never have been much of a "good-time boy," and this is certainly not improving that aspect of my personality.

I do appreciate how openhanded people have been with their care and support. It really is true that one of the greatest gifts that you can give someone who is hurting is simply "presence"—not advice, not presents, not tokens of affection (though who doesn't like to be reminded that they are loved!) and not even unbidden help—but just "presence," or the sense that you are remembering and thinking of the other. I often find myself opening an email, reading a note here on CaringBridge, or receiving a card and just deeply and genuinely smiling because it is *so* good to be remembered—and usually prayed for.

With the morning light and today's possibilities, I am singing "10,000 Reasons" by Matt Redman, truly hoping that my song will last until evening.

WELCOMING VERSUS SEIZING

Two months ago I could well have imagined spending time on CaringBridge with updates and prayers for friends. But I never would have imagined writing my own cancer journal.

In a small flash, the focus of daily attention has changed from the routines and treats of family life, the preparations for business travel and the anticipation of holidays on the horizon, to

- management of hourly personal medical interventions
- triage of mundane items such as bills
- curiosity about what my strength might allow in daily interaction and activity

Life is just plain different now.

I like parts of my previous life better. But the choices have changed. Every day has always been an opportunity for attentiveness, gratitude and living into God's call. But today, on my sixty-sixth birthday, I have much less of a desire to "seize the day" and a greater desire to welcome it—with all its twists and turns, surprises and disappointments, moments of delight and discoveries of yet other areas to which I must pray my goodbyes and let the grieving roll.

I have felt reasonably good over the weekend—and that has provided the opportunity for some very special times with friends with whom we have shared life for well over four decades, and today with siblings, nephews, children, grandchildren and others in the "clan." Occasionally I slip away for a little rest, but mostly I've been able to enjoy the laughter, the wonder and the honesty of not avoiding the questions that kids want to ask and that adults often find awkward. There are no taboo subjects around here.

So today, on my sixty-sixth birthday, I'm living into whatever today's version of my "calling" is. I'm going to be as curious, as attentive, as genuinely joyful and as grateful for every hug and every pill as God gives me the grace to be.

Joyfully, Steve

God is shining and speaking so deeply in your words that I don't know how to express it. Thank you for taking the time and the energy in this journey to allow us to be a part of it, and to gain something of the gift of wisdom that is flowing through you with so much power in the midst of physical challenge. I will try to welcome this day.

JOHN ORTBERG

Sharol *June 26*

HEALTH UPDATE: Yesterday was the beginning of the third round of chemo. All went well as Steve was cared for by the wonderful oncology nurses at Emory. Steve is currently on the pump for forty-six hours as the third drug drips into his system. Nausea continues to be the most difficult side effect, though he finds if he holds very still, it is better. Steve lost quite a bit of weight during the last couple of weeks, so we're also pushing snacks to see if he can keep his weight up.

TRAVELING MERCIES

I often feel like a little girl who keeps asking, Where are we going? How long will it take to get there? What will it be like?

I know that allowing these questions to remain unanswered is what trust and faith is all about. And I do sense God's gentle care and reassurance of his presence as I want to see around the corner and cannot. But I still want to know!

In the midst of these questions, the Bible story that keeps coming to mind is from 2 Kings 6, where the king of Aram—who is furious with the prophet Elisha for telling the king of Israel the Aramean battle plans—sends his armies with their chariots and horses to surround the city where Elisha lives. The next morning, Elisha's servant gets up and outside sees enemy horses, chariots and armies everywhere and asks in a panic, "What will we do now?"

Elisha responds, "'Do not be afraid, for there are more with us than there are with them.' Then Elisha prayed: 'O LORD, please open his eyes that he may see.' So the LORD opened the eyes of the servant, and he saw; the mountain was full of horses and chariots of fire all around Elisha" (2 Kings 6:16-17).

I think that the Lord is saying to me, "Open your eyes and see my armies of faithful friends and angels and chariots of fire that are around you and Steve and your families, colleagues and all those dear to you." So that is my prayer—"open my eyes and let me see." It reminds me that we are not alone, that the battle is not ours but God's.

> *Your image of being in the car and wondering what is around the next bend reminded me of Anne Lamott saying that when driving at night our headlights show us just what is in front of us and miraculously that is enough to keep us going on our way. Prayers ascending.*
>
> MARY ANONA STOOPS

Basically God asks me and us to "stand still, and see the victory of the LORD on your behalf" (2 Chronicles 20:17)—one day at a time.

A QUIETER HEART

It's the fifth day of my current chemo treatment cycle, the day that my medication regimen changes and I go to "recovery" mode for the current cycle, hoping that my energy will begin to return before the next set, which will begin July 9. But I realized this morning that it is also the day that I am thinking about perseverance, persistence, patience and endurance.

I used to have a placard on my wall that read "Nothing Good Happens Fast." Eventually I took it down, because I realized that sometimes really good things do happen fast. But in our culture we have often expected, and pleaded for, and even demanded quick solutions, quick fixes and quick results. We get impatient. We lose interest otherwise.

But there is much to be learned in the disciplines of waiting, watching and longing. And, after all, it is our character that is being built during these periods, which is more important than the immediate physical solutions anyway.

The last few days physically have been okay. They haven't been great. The nausea has lessened somewhat, I am managing the fatigue and I have been mostly out of bed every day. I have been able to do a little reading and work. But the most important part of these days for me has been feeling the impatience rising and then heeding the other internal voice, which tells me to settle back in—to allow my heart to become quieter and more peaceful again—and to be grateful for the waiting.

Honestly, I don't know what this new spirit of quiet will bring (or even if I will manage to learn it in my normally fast, active world), or what it will ultimately accomplish in my life. But for today, it seems important to listen and to lean into the joy (and discipline) of this unhurried moment. "Be still, my soul."

Steve *July 6*

HEALTH UPDATE: Earlier this past week, the nausea was as bad as it's been. Sharol was able to talk with several of the members of the team at the Winship Cancer Institute. They decided to change the timing on how I am taking various medications and also to adjust one of the medications. The result of all of this is that I have had significantly less nausea since Thursday and none in the last two days. Part of this may also be due to the fact that I am now in the days in the treatment cycle when my energy, appetite and overall vitality should be improving substantially so that I am ready for the next round.

UNEXPECTED GIFTS

I'm grateful for a few days of feeling healthier. It amazes me when I read the stories of people who continue to live quite "normally" through all of this. The ups and downs in my day-to-day ability to function are pretty clear. So it's nice now to have days strung together where I can be out of bed the entire day, go for short walks, interact with a little desk work and be able to report honestly that "I'm feeling okay!" when asked how I'm doing.

As to other physical markers: I am not losing my hair, but apparently only about 11 percent of people on this particular regimen lose hair as a side effect. My weight continues to drop. I am now holding at about 130 pounds, a good 25 pounds below my "normal" weight. All of my blood counts and vitals remain in normal ranges.

I am in no pain—or more accurately, the pain that often accompanies this type of cancer is being well-managed. There are other interesting side effects, like hypersensitivity to touching anything cold, and very weird tastes and aftertastes to food, which are more irritating than problematic.

As the time it takes for me to bounce back from each treatment seems to get longer, it pushes my patience. But remembering that the physical aspects of this are only a part of the whole is helpful.

On days when the physical is particularly difficult, there is almost always some aspect of life and learning that brings joy and reminds me that gifts are to be found in the most unexpected places.

Sharol *July 9*

HEALTH UPDATE: The fourth round has begun. All in all, it's been a good day. Steve's lab results were better than expected, even better than two weeks ago. He's lost several more pounds but his energy and his attitude remain positive and strong. The long list of drugs and everything that treats the effects of the chemo have been infused, and Steve is now wearing the pump that is slowly dripping the last drug into his system for the next forty hours. He was able to eat a full dinner. And, after a day of sitting, we just walked around the block. Steve admits that he is stocking up on food and exercise because he probably won't feel like eating or moving much tomorrow. But the great news is that he feels like it today.

HUNTING FOR PEARLS

Steve was dreading this day and, like a boy headed to the dentist, prayed just to be brave. Having had three days where he experienced no nausea and had energy to walk almost a mile with me each evening, Steve is not very excited about the side effects that will undoubtedly strike in the coming days. But we also remain hopeful that the changes we made in Steve's meds during the last round will bear fruit in this one. Steve definitely earned the bravery badge today and now is working yet again on courage, endurance and perseverance.

This morning in a devotional I occasionally read, I discovered this quote by Jean Paul Richter: "The burden of suffering seems a tombstone hung around our necks, while in reality it is only the weight which is necessary to keep down the diver while he is hunting for pearls."

> *Perhaps the pearl of great price may only be found in deep waters. If only we could just pluck it while walking along the beach.*
>
> PRISCILLA LASMARIAS KELSO

Thank you for cheering us on and praying for us in this great hunt. The pearls we're finding are quite extraordinary.

Steve *July 12*

HEALTH UPDATE: It's Saturday afternoon, the fourth day of my fourth round of chemo. The "pump," which accompanies me for days two and three, was removed yesterday. In the last rounds, days four and five were the hardest days for side effects. Today, however, I seem to be doing okay. The new regimen of how I take my medications seems to be helping especially with the nausea, but I am also convinced that I am being sustained by the community that prays.

HEALING IN THE QUIET

The fatigue is high, but I'm just giving in to the need for rest.

Healing is encouraged in the quiet moments.

Steve *July 16*

HEALTH UPDATE: A little later today I am scheduled to have an MRI, the first of several assessments to determine whether the chemotherapy of the last two months is having any real effect.

PRAYING FOR HEALING

One person told me how disturbing it is to her to watch so many thousands of prayers on my behalf and yet (so far) to see minimal physical evidence of healing.

Does God really heal?

Are the "prayers of the righteous" effective?

Does God listen to the desires of our hearts?

Does the amount of prayer have any special impact?

Honestly, while I understand the importance and logic of questions like this—and many others—most of these questions are not ones that are important to me.

I truly don't know what God has planned. None of us really knows what the physical symptoms of my cancer will be over time. I could receive "healing" through whatever means, or I could continue to deteriorate. Of course, what we would love to see is significant healing. With God, nothing is impossible, and

I would certainly welcome a miraculous intervention.

But life is about a lot more than physical health. It is measured by a lot more than medical tests and vital signs.

More important than the more particular aspects of God's work with us (in the physical, social, psychological, spiritual, mental realms of life) is God's overall presence with us, nourishing, equipping, transforming, empowering and sustaining us for whatever might be God's call for us today.

Today, my call might be to learn something new about rest.

Today, my call might be to encourage another person in some very tangible way.

Today, my call might be to learn something new about patience, endurance and identification with those who suffer.

Today, my call might be to mull through a new insight about God's truth or character.

The prayers and support of people along the way are also about God's call to each of them (and me!) *today*. As people pray, we are all changed, and we are all called to focus in a new way. We are all changed as individuals and as a community.

Yes, I'm really eager to know what is happening in my body to this cancer. I'm hopeful that the report about my tumor will be a "good" one and that it might portend a more physically healthy future. But whatever we find out over the next days, I am more eager that it would help me to be more attentive, more grateful, more loving, more joyful and more gracious.

I saw a bumper sticker yesterday that I loved: "More wagging; less barking!" At that moment I was grumbling inside because it was so hard just to complete my short walk in the neighborhood. But almost immediately my perspective changed. Grumbling was changing nothing, but a fresh infusion of joy could color the world.

HEALTH UPDATE: It's been three months since I was diagnosed with aggressive metastatic pancreatic cancer. Because I was in such good physical condition at the beginning of this unexpected journey, I have been able to handle the most intensive prescribed regimen of chemotherapy. The doctors have determined from the MRI that I have had marginal shrinkage in the primary tumor on my pancreas, an indication that they are holding the cancer at bay on that front. However, the tests also revealed that the cancer has spread farther throughout my liver and that overall, the treatments have been only marginally effective.

HOW GOD ANSWERS PRAYER

The cancer continues to have the upper hand.

What now seems clear from a purely physical perspective is that in all probability the remainder of my life on this earth is now to be counted in weeks and months. This was not completely unexpected news for either Sharol or me. We have known all along that this cancer is virulent and aggressive. We feel good that we have given it a strong fight from what is available from medical science. I have an exceptional oncology team and an even better team of those who are continuing to pray and to support us in this battle.

As we move forward, our purpose is to balance further medical interventions with issues related to the quality of my life. For example, if I continue a really aggressive approach to therapy, I may well expect that my day-to-day life will be compromised significantly (as it has been) by the side effects of the treatment. If, on the other hand, we begin eliminating some of those therapies that are causing the more enervating side effects, I may well be shortening this chapter of my life by a few days or weeks. Of course it is impossible to tell either way with any certainty, so all of our decision making is a walk of faith and careful discernment in the counsel of other wise and faithful advisers and practitioners.

Our short-term plan is to begin a different chemotherapy regimen that has the potential of slowing the growth of the cancer and even holding it in check. It has proven effective in cancers like mine and has fewer side effects than the very aggressive regimen that I have been on. I will go in for a chemo infusion each Wednesday for three weeks in a row and then have a week off. At the end of two full cycles there will be another time of full evaluation.

These are the mere facts. This past weekend we were able to be together as an immediate family (children and grandchildren) to share all of this, to weep together, to laugh and lament, and to pray.

Cancer is an in-your-face reminder of the nature of our broken world. None of this is the way that God intended for life to be, and yet it is one part of destiny that we will all share one day.

There is a much bigger story of which this is only a tiny part. And it is God's story of love, hope, forgiveness, reconciliation and joy. We went into this journey choosing to trust God and to offer our fears to God. We've been so grateful for the freedom from fear and the abundance of peace that we have experienced. There are, of course, times of discouragement, grief, pain and wonder. After all, there are a lot of unknowns ahead of us.

Many are praying for one of God's "big" miracles. We are as well. But it is not how God answers prayer that determines our response to God.

God is committed to my ultimate healing. But being cured of my cancer may or may not be a part of that healing work.

Joyfully, Steve

Sharol *July 24*

WALKING TOGETHER

We had such a memorable time with our adult children and our grandchildren this past weekend—lots of laughter, lots of tears, lots of conversation. On Saturday afternoon, with all the grandchildren next door, Steve was able to tell the story of his (and our) cancer journey. Though we have filled in the details for each of our kids along the way, we have not been together since Easter, when Steve first noticed symptoms.

Our friends Stuart and Mary Banks Knechtle, who have walked with us from the beginning, were also with us to answer questions and remind us that "in life and in death, we belong to God," and that Jesus said to a grieving sister, "I am the resurrection and the life. Those who believe in me, even though they die, will live, and everyone who lives and believes in me will never die" (John 11:25-26).

In varying degrees and in different ways, we are all sad, angry, disappointed and shocked.

My argument with God is all about the waste of this (what I perceive to be) valuable life in the kingdom of God. Why not allow Steve more years of fruitful ministry and relationships? We have been a team now for over forty-one years and we are good together. Why break that up now?

Last week, I was reading a portion of Matthew 26 where,

after observing a young woman pouring out super valuable perfume on Jesus' feet, Jesus' disciples muttered, "Why this waste?" Jesus responded that she had provided a good service for him—and that is what mattered. I imagine that when Jesus was crucified and buried the disciples again muttered, "Why this waste?"

And yet, without this waste, we would never know life as it was meant to be lived, life with eternal significance, and death robbed of its sting and hopelessness. Because of Jesus' death, we can have life, abundant and eternal life. In the past months, I have muttered, "Why this waste?" and yet I am reminded that in God's hands nothing is ever wasted.

Thank you for praying for all of us as we have questions and fears along the way. We wonder what the next weeks and months will be like. We still pray for healing, real physical healing here and now. But we pray even more for the deep kind of shalom healing for Steve, for our family and for all of you who are walking with us. We are grateful to be seeing some of that already.

Last Sunday night, our five-year-old granddaughter, Anna, asked her mom and dad when she might get her regular grandpa back.

This led to a conversation with Anna and seven-year-old Claire about Papa's prognosis and the new body that Jesus would give him in heaven.

Anna said, "I wish I knew if Jesus was going to heal him here or in heaven. I think I do at least. But I know that Jesus keeps his promises. We can trust him."

Well said, Anna.

We're choosing to trust Jesus.

HEALTH UPDATE: Tomorrow I begin a new regimen of chemotherapy. It has the possibility of slowing or arresting the progression of my cancer without quite so many side effects. I have now had three full weeks with no chemo and am feeling so much more energetic that I hate to start chemo again. I've even regained a few pounds. And yet it is important to balance the quality of my life with the therapeutic need to continue to fight the cancer cells that are still multiplying and spreading.

THINKING ABOUT THE FUTURE

Someone asked me this week what I planned to do in the months ahead. I really didn't have an answer except to say that I am *not* planning to focus on any projects that I somehow feel are being "expected" of me. For example, several people have suggested that I write a book, and they have a lot of opinions on what they would like me to write about. But honestly, there is not much joy for me in writing.

I would rather focus on other kinds of creative projects, like our house remodeling. Sharol and I have decided to keep and to remodel the home that we own here in Decatur (now we live in the president's house on the Columbia Theological Seminary campus). Our house will be a great place for Sharol to live in the years ahead, and we have the time now to get it back into good shape.

I also have a number of lists of things that I want to finish, like giving away my library in creative and productive ways, finally disposing of old and useless files, and engaging with students, faculty and staff in our Columbia community.

I have some people that I am hoping to see.

And, of course, I still have a number of deep human and global concerns for which I want to do my part in helping with the healing.

There is a kind of daily "calling" to which I want to be attentive. Some days this will include more active options, while other days I will likely only have energy for quieter possibilities.

Sharol *July 30*

HEALTH UPDATE: Today is day two of the first round of the new chemo regimen. Though very tired, Steve has been up, able to eat and able to interact with the grandkids, who spent much of the day with us. Hopefully now, with each day, Steve will gain strength and energy and be ready for the second treatment next Wednesday.

FEASTING IN THE VALLEY

We continue to be grateful for your prayers and good wishes. Every day these prayers are being answered as we experience amazing peace and courage. This can only be the work of the Holy Spirit.

Recently I sat with friends as we studied Psalm 23. I've always separated this familiar psalm into three somewhat unrelated scenarios: first, the beautiful meadow, rich in green grass and quiet waters, an idyllic place of peace and rest, free of distraction and hardship; second, the valley of the shadow of death, where the Shepherd's rod and staff protect the sheep; and third, an abundant feast in the presence of enemies.

But at this time in my life, I read Psalm 23 differently. I wonder if the valley of the shadow of death is also where we are treated to an abundant meal even though surrounded by enemies.

I wonder if it is in that same shadowed valley where the Shepherd offers rest in green pastures, beside still waters.

Perhaps we lack nothing, not in the idyllic destination, but in the place of darkness, pain and suffering where the Shepherd provides rest and healing.

Steve and I are discovering that we truly lack nothing and are finding peaceful rest in the valley of pancreatic cancer and chemo.

The Shepherd is so faithful.

We are grateful.

Sharol *August 6*

HEALTH UPDATE: Today was a chemo day—an uneventful process of labs, doctor's appointment and infusion. Steve's white blood cell count, a concern with this new regimen, was actually stronger than last week. And there was more great news. Steve gained about six pounds this week. Food is tasting better, and while Steve is not hungry, he is eating. He has felt drained of energy today because of the chemo drugs, but we are hopeful that he will be able to attend the Columbia Seminary board of trustees meeting tomorrow.

RECEIVING

I am giving thanks for so many gifts these days. Friends and family along with our church community have rallied around us in unexpected ways, offering help of all kinds along with prayers, food and well wishes. We are also grateful to be part of this amazing seminary community. A large portion of the faculty met on our patio last week to catch up and hear the latest about our journey. These gifted men and women are not just academic colleagues but are dear friends who gathered around us and prayed for both of us. We couldn't ask for a more committed group of friends.

The faculty and Steve's cabinet are moving forward as the new school year approaches, committed to building and encouraging imaginative and resilient pastors and leaders, rolling out a new curriculum this fall instead of slipping into a kind of malaise, which often hits when a leader is incapacitated. We couldn't be more thankful or proud. Students and staff are also joining hands to support us. We only wish we could be a part of their lives during this season. We are also blessed with gifted men and women on our board of trustees who have pledged their support in a rich variety of ways. How grateful we are for these leaders who are committed not only to us and to Jesus Christ, but also to the future of CTS.

May the Lord continue to give
you every good gift.
May your hands and hearts
remain open to receive.
May you enjoy the fullness of
our Creator,
who is the prayer-hearing God.

ALISON SIEWERT

Last Sunday, our son Chip and his wife, Kristen, and their children, along with our longtime friend Alex Gee from Madison, Wisconsin, "had church" in our family room. We read 2 Corinthians 9:6-12 several times (an unusual passage of Scripture, perhaps, but part of my daily reading), asking first what word or phrase stood out, then asking how the Spirit was speaking into our lives, and finally listening for God's invitation to each of us.

In a season where we are majoring in receiving rather than in giving or serving, I had to admit that God is inviting me to simply open my hands and receive the life, the gifts and the peace that God wants to give me.

It's a place of humility.

It's a place of gratitude.

But it's also a place of profound joy.

I can only say thank you.

Steve *August 7*

HEALTH UPDATE: I'm tired, but have very few other side effects from my chemo treatment yesterday. I'm thankful.

FEELING THE RIPPLES

Today I am taking some time to read through more of the many, many cards and letters that have come our way. The surprising part for me is the stories that people have taken the time to share of the ways in which our lives have intersected and the surprising ways in which God has used those encounters.

Among the letters was a poem by Dr. Steve Moore (who directs the M. J. Murdock Charitable Trust), written on Memorial Day in 2012. It is moving to me, especially in reading all these stories from others. Here's an excerpt from it.

The Ripple

Where the ripple goes,
No one can fully know.

Sometimes the wave
gently washes over with only a whisper.
Other times the motion dislodges even that which
seemed so firm.

The choice, the whim, the urge,
the hope, the fear, the move so slight and small.
What brings the ripple?
It's often hard to know. . . .

Our lives do ripple then recede.
Though often unaware, we hope
for good and cast our lives
to things and those we love.
And pray the ripple grows and goes.

There are so many ripples, and so many memories. Having quiet spaces to reflect and sit in simple gratitude is a privilege.

Steve *August 13*

HEALTH UPDATE: It's quiet in the chemotherapy infusion bay this morning. Often there are up to eight patients—all of us sitting in the hospital equivalent of a recliner and receiving the various scheduled medications through a series of intravenous tubes. The chemo nurses hover between patients, setting up for various procedures and attaching more fluids to put in our bodies.

DAILY ROUTINE

This morning I am feeling quite good, even though it was a relatively difficult week. This regimen of chemo seems to have fewer side effects, but also seems to be more cumulative. In other words, each week seems to be harder than the last. Perhaps that's why I will get two weeks off after today. My body needs a longer recovery time from the exhaustion and the achy feelings that keep me on the couch or on my bed for longer stretches of time. I wish that I had the energy to see more people or attend to a few more little projects, but I just don't.

Sharol and I were able to meet yesterday with the man whom we are likely to hire as the contractor on our house remodeling project. We liked him a lot. His values seem to line up with our own as we think about what needs to be done to the house. The next step will be to move into a "design phase," where the company will work with us on drawings for a remodeled bathroom and a possible carport for this eighty-five-year-old bungalow. This house was our home before we moved into the president's house on campus over five years ago, and will be Sharol's (and perhaps my) home once again after the remodeling is complete.

Our seminary board meeting at the end of last week, which focused on the future leadership in my absence, was exceptional. Not only was the conversation deeply supportive of us and eager to help us in every way, but it was full of wisdom and vision as the trustees considered the days ahead. It would be easy to move into a sort of transitional or holding mode, but the board is committed (as are the faculty and staff) to moving aggressively ahead with the revised curriculum and with various other academic and physical projects on campus. The plan is that Dr. Deb Mullen, our academic dean and executive vice president, will continue to be acting president through September. She has served wonderfully in that role ever since I got sick back in April, continuing to fulfill her own responsibilities as well as mine. The board has also appointed a committee to identify an interim president to serve until a presidential search can be concluded (probably by next summer). It is a bit uncertain what role I will have in these months, although more than likely, I will have to request moving to full-time disability.

Well, as I sit here the nurses just came by to tell me that my white blood cell and hemoglobin levels are both a little low. This is one of the possible side effects of this chemo regimen. They will now have to check with the doctors to see if they can treat me or whether we will have to skip treatment this week.

Ah, the word just came back that I'm "good to go," so now I will join the others around me with a bouquet of tubes. Because of my low blood numbers, we will have to be especially careful about infections over the next weeks. We are pretty good already with washing hands and using hand sanitizer, but this may mean even fewer visitors too. And the low counts probably account for the extra fatigue that I have been experiencing.

This is a glimpse of a few of the pieces of my daily routine. We don't always know what to anticipate and we approach each day with open hands and with gratitude. It's all we can do. But it's enough.

Steve *August 16*

HEALTH UPDATE: On my current chemo regimen, the second full day after infusion has been the hardest. Yesterday was no exception. Sharol came home from a teaching commitment last night and discovered that I had a significant fever. She called the twenty-four-hour cancer help line at the Cancer Institute and was told that I needed to come in to the emergency room. So, at 10:30 last night, Doug Taylor (faithful friend and next-door neighbor) chauffeured us to the emergency room at Emory Hospital, where we spent the next four hours. After testing, it was finally decided that it was "safer" for me to be at home than to admit me to the hospital, where I might be exposed to something. The final diagnosis was that this was just a spike in my temperature due to the chemo. Sharol is over at the seminary teaching now, and I'm sure she is exhausted. I'm really praying for energy, wisdom and clarity for her today. She is such a fine teacher, but can easily lose her confidence at times like this.

THE WORK OF HEAVEN

Our kids and grandkids are all coming to see me later today. These visits are wonderfully encouraging. There is something about a house filled with the laughter of little children that can heighten the sense of joy. And after all, "Joy is the serious business of Heaven"!

Steve *August 20*

WHAT WERE YOU EXPECTING?

When people see me for the first time these days, they often have funny looks on their faces. When I ask, they acknowledge that I look thinner than they had anticipated (after all, I am now more than twenty-five pounds lighter than I was four months ago), or that they are surprised that I'm not bald. It seems that being bald has become one of the universal signs of cancer since it obviously is one of the more visible side effects of many kinds of chemotherapy. Since I have already had a number of weeks of aggressive chemotherapy, many people expect me to be bald.

So far my hair has remained intact. I wasn't expecting the experience of two days ago when I was washing my hair in the shower and suddenly found that I had a mouthful of hair. At first, I didn't even understand what was happening, but when I looked at my hands, which had been lightly massaging my scalp, I realized that my hair was coming out in clumps. So for the last couple of days I've looked a little like I have been rolling around with a shedding dog. My polo shirts and pillowcases have been covered with shedding hair.

Because I didn't lose any hair with the more aggressive chemo regimen, this was simply something that I had not expected for this round either. Of course it's not painful, but it's another reminder of how shaped we are in our daily lives by our expectations. We assume that our days will have certain patterns, schedules and activities associated with them. We assume that what we have anticipated about our lives will in fact come to fruition. If life turns out to be different than we expected, even in some of the finer details, it throws us off and introduces various amounts of insecurity, loss of control, or anxiety.

Even hair loss can do that. It's not that I am overly upset about my hair loss—or even whether this will result in merely a "thinning" effect or a more billiard ball style—but rather that it's another reminder that I'm not in control and that there are surprises that await me that I cannot anticipate.

Every time I find myself saying, "This is not the way that it's supposed to be!" I have to respond by asking, "And why do I assume that it's supposed to be this way?"

Unmet or unfulfilled expectations can demand higher energy depletion than they are worth. The fact is, our expectations are generally built on what is simply familiar to us or on our anticipations around our heart's desires, and there are no guarantees in life that we can be assured about either.

Circumstances change.

Relationships change.

Adjustments have to be made.

Times of both acute and chronic disease are times when lots of adjustments have to be made daily. We can either resist or we can surrender. The act of surrender doesn't mean that we give up looking for the best, but rather that we let go of expending energy on trying to maintain that which is slipping or being ripped away. Instead, we "pray our goodbyes" to what has been, we open our hearts to what is new and we walk again toward the place of gratitude, attentiveness and learning that nurtures energy and finally results in joy.

Steve's cancer haircut

So, I'm losing my hair. It's annoying. It's messy. Maybe I'll give myself the buzzcut of my childhood. But this time I'll also remind myself that it's just another broken expectation and that I have a choice about how I respond. Expectations only hurt us when they hold us captive. When we can let go, a whole world of possibilities can emerge.

HEALTH UPDATE: Today is day two of this first of three treatments before a CT scan and an MRI to see if this regimen is working. This round is difficult as Steve is again experiencing the cumulative effects of previous treatments, which means some numbness in his feet and ankles, loss of energy, and a general malaise throughout his body. Gratefully there is no nausea.

THE POWER OF REMEMBERING

There's nothing glamorous about chemotherapy. We remarked yesterday that it gets harder and harder to choose this journey when Steve feels pretty good the day before and morning of chemo and then in a matter of hours leaves the infusion bay feeling sick and drained of energy.

We've had several days with good friends, telling stories, watching movies and hanging out together. Steve and I are struck with the power of storytelling and its vivid reminders of the people and experiences that have shaped us. Stories are also reminders of the ways that God has been at work—often surprising us with unexpected grace when we didn't know we needed it.

When we remember God's faithfulness in confusing, daunting or even impossible situations, it strengthens our trust in the triune God who is the same yesterday, today and forever. We're counting on that as we move through this challenging season.

Thanks to many of you for sharing with us the stories of the ways that the Spirit has been at work in your lives, sometimes through a word Steve spoke or a time when the Spirit simply showed up. We marvel at God's ability to take the little we have to offer and then do wonderful things in the lives of others.

We continue to live with gratitude, trust and joy, knowing that the choice to do so is made easier when remembering the God who pulled us through in the past.

Steve *September 3*

HEALTH UPDATE: Today was supposed to be chemo day, but my lab tests this morning indicated that my white blood cell count has fallen too low and this week's treatment has needed to be postponed. In our view this is not bad news, since I'm not feeling well anyway. But it does put us off schedule for the next MRI and CT scans. I'm sure it will all work out. In the meantime, having a little distance from the chemo will hopefully provide my body a chance for some healing. Of course, the prayer is that the cancer will not take this as an opportunity to grow at the same time.

DEPRESSION

There have been several times in my life when Sharol or a friend asked, "Are you depressed?" Sharol is asking the question again.

"Are you depressed?" I don't know. Maybe.

Depression is hard to measure. It comes in so many shades and levels with so many varying symptoms. But it is most often marked by a kind of apathy toward life.

I do know that this is a darker time for me as the accumulative side effects of the chemo extend further into every week, as the fatigue confines me for longer periods to my bed or the couch, and as the general sense of feeling rotten clouds my days. It's definitely not a happy time.

Despite a common view that a person can simply "will" his or her way out of darkness, it is generally not that simple. Depression includes a complex cluster of chemical and psychological components.

So maybe I'm struggling with depression. It isn't extreme—more the garden variety, I suspect—but it's the only way that I can describe what I have been feeling.

Living in the darkness means that I have to shift gears. And I don't like having to do that. I don't mind slowing down, but to shift into a mode where the best that I can do is to listen to something from the Internet or TV, to pray, or to have a very short text conversation with a friend is discouraging.

I'm not experiencing this every day, but I am experiencing it with increasing regularity right now. I'm hoping that this is temporary and that I will see some recovery once this current series of chemo is over. When I am not on chemo, I feel so much better. But, of course, during these times I also don't know how the cancer is continuing to progress.

So what is there to do in the dark times? The first thing is not to be afraid or embarrassed to identify it. Unfortunately, in our culture there is still a kind of shame connected with depression, as if we should never experience it. And after all, I'm the guy who signs every letter with "joyfully." But joy is dependent on who I am and how I am loved more than on my circumstances. It is happiness that takes the hit when circumstances go bad. Not joy.

Our circumstances are just too variable to be the foundation of our daily feelings about life. It is too easy to equate "blessing" with circumstances instead of with God's loving embrace. The fact is, I'm blessed because I belong to God—in life, in death and in everything in between—not because my circumstances are always the way that I want them to be.

Identifying that this is a dark time simply acknowledges the truth of my life, but says little about the condition of my heart. But truth always opens the door to new life, so I would rather face darkness full on than try to put on yet another happy mask.

The second thing that I'm doing in the darkness is letting God and God's people minister to me with the gifts that remind me of who I am and of God's forever presence. These are the gifts that range from music in the background, to the sight of carefree birds fluttering at the feeder outside our window; from the gentle words of a friend's favorite poet presented as an encouragement, to the faces of our faculty in a cherished group portrait that I just received; from the laughter of the grandchildren, to the touch of the hand of my wife or a dear friend. There are so many gifts that are meant to be included in the darkness as well as in the light and that bring special meaning in each space.

> *One day in a particularly low mood I came across a Puritan prayer called "Valley of Vision," which says, in part: "Lord, high and holy, meek and lowly, Thou has brought me to the valley of vision, where I live in the depths but see thee in the heights; . . . Lord, in the daytime stars can be seen from deepest wells, and the deeper the wells the brighter thy stars shine; Let me find thy light in my darkness, thy life in my death . . . thy glory in my valley." May our Lord's rich joy shine in your valley.*
>
> STAN OTT

And, by the way, I'm still joyful.

HEALTH UPDATE: While all my numbers were low last week, my white cell count was particularly problematic. The count is normally in the range of 8 to 10. The previous week my cell count had dropped to 6.6, but by last Wednesday it was at 2.7. This means, among other things, that my susceptibility to infection and disease is higher too.

THE GOOD WORK OF GOD

Today I simply wanted to let you know that these past few days have been quite encouraging. Not only have I felt better, both physically and emotionally, but my body is having a chance to rebuild. We'll see what my blood count is next Wednesday when I go back for chemo, but I wouldn't be surprised if my numbers were back at near-normal levels.

I have also been so encouraged with being strong enough this week to attend (albeit sitting in the back row a safe distance from the crowds) Columbia Seminary's 187th annual fall convocation. This is one of my favorite gatherings at Columbia, and it was so refreshing to be there to see the entering class welcomed, to watch the faculty in their medieval academic garb pledge their support to these new students, and to participate in the commitment of the staff to make Columbia the best learning environment possible.

I have also been so encouraged in the last days by messages of support during the emotionally dark times. Today as Sharol and I worshiped at home, I could not help but thank God for how encouraged I feel today.

Whether circumstances are favorable or not, the good work of God does not cease.

Sharol *September 10*

HEALTH UPDATE: Just before noon today, Steve finished another chemotherapy treatment. Sadly, as we left the infusion bay, Steve already felt achy and out of sorts. We've got the drill down now. A good lunch of tortellini and ravioli because by dinner, he will only want scrambled eggs. Because Steve didn't have a treatment last week due to low white cell counts, we wondered if next week's scheduled scans to assess the effectiveness of this regimen might be postponed until he had completed three treatments of this second round of Gemzar-Abraxane. The good news is that Steve will have the scans next week and no chemo! We take delight in small gifts these days.

SEASON OF SUFFERING

We continue to be amazed at the strength, endurance and encouragement that God has given us. Even in the hard times, we discover grace and mercy. In a strange way, I'm grateful for this season of suffering as it reminds us on whom we rely for strength and well-being. We also feel connected to so many around the world who are on their own difficult journeys.

When God says in 2 Corinthians 12:9, "My grace is sufficient for you, for power is made perfect in weakness," we say a loud "Amen." It's definitely true.

DO NOT RESUSCITATE

When a friend suggested we get a "Do Not Resuscitate" bracelet for my dad, my breath caught sharply in my throat. *It might as well say "Choose Death,"* I thought. How could we ever choose death over life?

My dad is living with terminal cancer that is aggressively eating his abdomen. He has lost weight. The chemo has killed his hair. When I visit, I notice how much slower he moves.

Back home, I notice that I move more slowly too. Cancer is pushing its way into our normal routines. I do laundry and think about questions that don't have answers.

My kids watch me cry while I cook. I'm sad that they will

Emilie and Steve

know the reality of death so early in life. I wonder if they will fear losing others as well.

I don't spend a lot of time wondering what God is trying to teach me when life is hard. I don't believe that God has set up my life as if it were a school curriculum that I might pass or fail. But I do think about how this situation fits with what I know about God, and I wonder how it will help to shape my kids' view of the world. I know there are plenty of lessons that I could teach them today:

- God redeems all things.
- God holds all our days in his hands.
- God is the very best doctor.

Mostly, though, I find myself repeating this ever-important truth to my kids and to myself: death hurts because we were made for life.

"I have set before you life and death," we read in Deuteronomy 30:19. "Choose life." Some would say that "choosing life" means choosing only to see the positive, looking always for the silver lining. To walk this path is to live in perpetual denial. Following Jesus means choosing to see the truth even when it is painful. Death hurts. Loss causes deep ache. And somehow in the agony of pain, we are free to find joy because we can trust that Jesus redeems all things.

Where death reminds us that we are made of dust, inconsequential in the course of history, Jesus reminds us that in him we are loved and have life forever. That is a reason to sing even on dark days. For me, choosing life means asking hard questions about suffering. Choosing life means admitting I'm angry and brokenhearted.

Although I could avoid the grief and teach my children to do the same, this would be a mistake. The path of freedom, I think, is to look death square in the eyes and proclaim, "I choose life."

HEALTH UPDATE: I don't need to go in for chemo today. Yesterday I had two important scans (CT and MRI) to determine whether this latest regimen of chemo has actually accomplished anything. We likely won't get the official results until the 24th when I visit the oncology team again. At that time, I presume that we will reassess how to manage the next chapter of cancer treatment. I honestly don't have a clue as to what will happen next.

ETERNAL LIFE

Sometimes these days, I can't help myself. My mind just moves in these theological circles. Maybe it's a side effect of feeling better.

I've been thinking about eternal life, which is defined in the Bible quite differently than we often define heaven in our secular imaginations. Eternal life in the Bible is defined as the present reality of knowing God as revealed in Jesus. In John 17:3 Jesus prays, "And this is eternal life, that they may know you, the only true God, and Jesus Christ whom you have sent." Especially through the Gospel of John it is clear that "eternal life" is to be considered the primary identity or state of a person who knows God. We have eternal life *now*, not only as an expectation for the future.

One of the hardest realities about eternal life seen this way is that our experience of eternal life is almost always in transition. Our lives and our perceptions are constantly changing as we grow and develop.

I choose to call all of these transitions, particularly the bigger ones, "conversions," precisely because they signal the movement from one understanding or way of being to another.

Our first conversion in eternal life may be identified in our initial steps toward some sort of change in our relationship with Jesus. At some point Jesus becomes more than a name to us, or a mere historical figure, and we begin to relate to Jesus as a friend, or as Savior and Lord. That is indeed conversion and is often the movement in our lives that people describe as "conversion" or "being born again."

But that's not the end of it. There are lots of other conversions that continue to occur in our lives. In my experience there have been many big changes in my understanding of my relationship with God, and I see these as conversions—as a remodeling of my faith and friendship with Jesus. Most of these conversions have been accompanied by struggles of some sort. Most have not been easy because they are about transitions, and that often means transition from what is familiar to places that are more unknown and somewhat frightening. What am I giving up? Am I "losing" my faith because I am launching into unknown territory? Why is this happening to me? What will others think if they find out how much I am changing? And the questions go on.

At this present stage of my life, I am approaching another big transition. I am now in the process of moving from life to Life—or to being "swallowed up by life," as Paul describes the transition through physical death in 2 Corinthians 5:4.

As I get closer to this big "conversion," I am discovering other transitions along the way—changes in how I view suffering, time, relationships, grief, calling and so many other things. Conversions are happening in my life, and, I assume, they will continue to happen until the moment of my final conversion. Or perhaps my movement from life to Life won't be the final change. Maybe there is a lot more.

All of that is still ahead of me, and I have confidence that it will be nothing short of spectacular.

Steve *September 24*

HEALTH UPDATE: This morning we met with my oncology team at the Winship Cancer Institute at Emory. Here is the *really* good news: The scans revealed that this latest regimen of chemotherapy has been successful in halting the spread of the cancer. The cancer in my liver has receded (the smaller lesions are gone altogether), and the primary tumor in my pancreas has continued to decrease in size. The scans could find no more cancer throughout the rest of my abdomen or lungs. The cancer has regressed some in the last three months. When you add in the facts that I have regained some weight and have seen some improvement in my muscle tone and energy levels, it is a fair assessment to say that I am physically "better." Even though this is not a cancer that is curable or that will go into remission, it is really nice to know that for now we have been able to stop the cancer from growing. Since the current regimen of chemo is working we will essentially hold the course with treatments every week or two as I am able to tolerate them. They will do lab tests weekly to monitor what is happening.

WHAT I CAN CHOOSE

The journey with terminal cancer has many dimensions. There are certainly the physical concerns about what is happening in my body. But there are also relational, psychological, vocational and spiritual dimensions. Every day I/we are contending with the changes that are taking place in our lives. Every day I am asking myself not only how I am feeling physically, but how should I be using the gift of this day. I remind myself that my primary identity is *not* as a cancer patient, but rather as a beloved child of God. My call is to learn, to grow and to follow. It is to empty myself of my expectations, my ambitions and my pride, and instead to allow myself to be filled with hope, love, faith and joy, which are then shaped into gifts for today.

Today's conversation with the doctor suggests that I might have longer to enjoy this life than we were originally expecting. I may indeed get to participate in another Christmas. I may get to see our house remodeling project completed. I may be able to complete more of the items on my end-of-life lists. But whether I do or not is clearly not the point.

> *In this life, we are all terminal. Not to belittle your unique struggles, but to be reminded that the courage and faithfulness by which you travel this road is the same we all should be exercising—not an end-of-life journey, but one of taking up our cross daily and following in the footsteps of the one who brings wholeness, peace, and reconciles all things to himself.*
>
> ANDY WADE

I don't get to choose the finish line.

But I can choose how I will run this portion of the race—and whether I am willing to sing the song that God has placed in my heart for this day.

I can choose how I will interact with both God and those people who line my path.

I can choose gratitude over complaint, and grace over fear.

I can choose to grieve by turning my face toward God rather than my back.

My most important choices have little to do with my cancer treatment plan. But they have a lot to do with my heart and my humanity.

Steve *October 2*

MAKING THE MOST OF THE UPS AND DOWNS

We often experience life as a series of waves with lots of ups and downs. Along the way we have to figure out how to surf the crests and to rest in the troughs without allowing the bumps to wear us out.

Life this week has been that sort of up-and-down experience. Even with the good news from last week about the decrease in my cancer activity, I still had to go through the exhaustive process of the chemo treatment, which kept me mostly in bed for about four days. Once I started to feel better, Sharol needed to remind me that my energy would not immediately pop back. It takes time to rebuild strength and stamina. It was disappointing to have to cancel several appointments because I just didn't feel well enough.

Since I don't have chemo this week, I am working hard to rebuild my energy reserves. Next Monday and Tuesday Columbia Theological Seminary is hosting a couple of events to mark my transition out of the role of president. I want to be able to enjoy these events, to honor and thank so many who have prayed for me these past five months, and to affirm how delighted I am with the direction that leadership at Columbia is moving in through this surprising change of circumstances. The trustees are hosting a big dinner on Monday evening, and there is an all-campus lunch on Tuesday. I so want to surf these events with joy rather than having to endure them because my energy reserves are low. But that requires some conditioning on my part.

I continue in my commitment to live one day at a time and to embrace whatever my calling is for that day. But I am recognizing that while I can't always accurately predict what the days will hold for me, each day I can be "in training" for what will come. That's what I tell myself as I struggle to do limited exercise with my tiny weights or as Sharol walks me around the block to get my legs back in shape.

To be a disciple, who follows a person or strategic plan, takes discipline. It doesn't just happen. And for me, discipline, especially when I am depleted, isn't fun. Indeed, it can be laborious and painful. But it is necessary for the sake of what may lie ahead. Discipline today is my calling to the possibility of a brighter tomorrow.

So today, I am off for the first of my two walks. I've already lifted my little weights. And I have some work to do at cleaning out a few files. It's not a glamorous calling today, but it's the march up a hill on which I hope for an adventurous ride down in the next several days. So life in the valley can be a gift too.

Sharol *October 8*

HEALTH UPDATE: This is chemo day and we know what this means for the next days. Thanks for praying for relief from the side effects and a quick bounce back. Steve is feeling the cumulative effects of the chemotherapy, making the effects of each treatment more pronounced.

PREPARING FOR THE REST OF LIFE

The past couple of days have been filled with emotion as Steve was honored first at a wonderful dinner with the board and friends of Columbia Theological Seminary and then at a fun-filled luncheon on campus with the entire CTS community. All of our children and a few of our friends celebrated with us. We looked back on the past five years of Steve's presidency with joy, laughter, celebration, gratitude and some tears, and looked ahead to the future of the seminary with great hope and anticipation. Thankfully, Steve felt healthy enough to enjoy both events and capped off both programs with his reflections and encouragement to the community to keep moving forward under the capable leadership that has been put in place. It was fun to watch him be strong and "presidential." We felt so loved and honored by those who came from near and far.

It is bittersweet. Out of all his work experiences, serving CTS as president was his favorite job. I, too, have loved the opportunity to welcome the CTS community into our home and to invest in those around us. It is definitely sad to see this chapter come to a close. But because it's been five months since Steve's diagnosis, the passages marked by this week's celebrations seem less monumental.

What has struck us is the suddenness with which life radically changed five months ago. On Good Friday, Steve was in the office, and by Tuesday, we were at Emory Hospital where an ultrasound and a CT scan revealed the presence of a mass on Steve's pancreas. Since that day, Steve has not been able to work more than an hour or two at a time. He's not been to church nor boarded an airplane. He's not been to the gym, something he did many times a week, nor has he been able to read an entire book.

Life is like that. Things happen that we do not expect or want. Friends often confess to me that they could never live as we are, embracing our changing circumstances, choosing to trust God with the outcome. "Our faith is not as strong as yours," they say. I've thought the same thing when observing the suffering of a friend or family member.

What Steve and I both realize is that we have been preparing all our lives for this season.

Our attempts to follow Jesus every day—every normal, mundane day—have prepared us for these tumultuous days.

This is what discipleship is all about.

Knowing that one of God's goals is to transform us to look more and more like Jesus, we have cultivated disciplines of prayer and Bible study while building community, pursuing justice and serving others. But more important, day by day the Spirit has been at work in us, chiseling away like a master sculptor. Chipping away what does not belong. Releasing the wonder of God's creation. Giving us confidence that our lives are safe in God's hands no matter what. We've been prepared to walk with confidence and hope—one step, one day at a time.

Gratefully, with the good report from Steve's scans two weeks ago, we continue to look eagerly to the future, embracing all the life offered to us. Our remodel plans have been submitted to the City of Decatur for permits, meaning that demolition will hopefully begin in the next week or two. We continue to draw much joy from this project.

HEALTH UPDATE: I don't have chemo again until October 22, so I get another week to recover. It seems as though it is taking longer for recovery from each of my chemo treatments now, so it is harder to plan my days and to anticipate how I will feel.

AWKWARD CONVERSATIONS

Conversations about death and dying are often awkward in our culture. We want to think more positively, or more optimistically. We want to be encouraging. For people of faith there is often the feeling that to talk about death is the opposite of talking about hope, and we want to be people who offer hope. Our awkwardness around the subject of death keeps us from considering our own deaths, or planning our funerals, or even making sure that we have written a will.

I've had many awkward conversations in the last five months with people who didn't want to talk about the probability that my cancer was "terminal." Others wanted to ask specific questions about my cancer or its treatment but were awkward about asking because they were embarrassed. It's not a polite subject.

I understand these and many other feelings about death. I've had them. I've been around people and didn't know how to ask them about what was going on physically and whether they were dying. I didn't know how they were responding spiritually or psychologically to their situation.

Now that I am the one living with the dying process on a daily basis, I am trying to help people around me feel more comfortable with it all. After all, why should death be an awkward topic? One of the Presbyterian creeds begins with the words, "In life and in death we belong to God." Believers of other times and cultures have often spoken about death with anticipation and even enthusiasm.

As my friend Tim Dearborn has said to me, "We either avoid talking about death or we overspiritualize it. So we allow its natural, normal, painful, even shattering—yet also nurturing—reality to slip past us."

While I want to live and to enjoy all that this life offers in relationships and opportunities for as long as possible, I also want to be as open about death as I can be. It is another important topic to be faced, discussed and embraced as just another phase of our living.

Steve *October 20*

FACING FEARS

I feel a little embarrassed talking about a fear that I have just identified. There are so many ultimate fears that I could have right now, and this one seems so petty. Nevertheless it has emerged, and like most fears needs to be faced.

My fear has to do with security in my day-to-day living. For over five months now I have been generally housebound. It's not that I don't go out of the house. I go over to the campus; I go for walks; I go to the hospital and to the doctor's office (though these excursions are not generally happy); and I have occasionally gone out for a meal. But my place of security is at home—close to Sharol, close to my bed, tethered to my familiar life patterns, my medications and all the things that give me comfort. When

I'm sick I just want to be home and close to the familiar.

As the days have progressed I now recognize that I've grown dependent. And with this dependence has come a fear of being away from home for too long. Thinking about travel for more than a few hours makes me anxious.

I've done a lot of traveling over the years, so these are new feelings and they have come quite unexpectedly. I feel foolish even admitting this reality.

As one who is staring old age in the face, I totally understand what you're saying. My challenges at the moment are nothing like the huge ones you are living with. But that need to have somebody nearby—and the occasional flickering thought, "What if something happens?"—are pretty similar. "It is not good for a person to be alone," especially when dealing with the hard things of life. This is vulnerability but not weakness. It's appropriate. And fortunately you have people who want you to lean on them without embarrassment or apology.

LINDA DOLL

But there it is.

I realized how afraid I was when I planned a whole day away with special friends this past Saturday. I looked forward to the day; I really enjoy these friends. But as the day approached I felt a growing anxiety. What if something happened? What if I got half through the day and didn't feel good? I felt a little out of control and more than a little dependent.

There are many little ways that life changes when you are facing sickness and death. I've now learned that new fears can pop up, along with a myriad of other challenges to the daily faithfulness to which I feel so strongly called. Things that have never bothered me much before may now feel like enemies.

So Saturday I faced a new fear. I spent all day with my friends, and I stared my fear in the face a number of times. When I returned home late in the evening, I realized that I had healed a little. My dear friends didn't know it, but their tender and thoughtful care was the love that was casting out my fear.

I wonder what other new surprises and fears I will discover in the weeks ahead, or how God will guide these unexpected bits of my complex journey. I want to come to the end with strength and courage. But life isn't always linear. There can be a jumble of twists and turns.

Maintaining my balance depends on my willingness to face the unexpected with humility and transparency, as well as endurance and fortitude. Stubborn pride is never a good companion. It only reinforces my anxieties.

Sharol *October 27*

GRACE COMES

The past five days have been very difficult for Steve. Each day, he's been in bed, eating because he needed to, not because he wanted to. He characterized Friday as the worst chemo day he has yet experienced. But today he is feeling more vigorous and has spent most of the day answering emails or working on projects. After our walk on campus and around the block, Steve still felt strong with no need of a nap. Today was a surprising gift of grace.

I've been thinking a lot about grace. You may have heard the story about the guy from the North who stopped at a Southern diner and ordered eggs and bacon. When his order came, the eggs and bacon were accompanied by a big helping of grits. "I didn't order grits," he told the waitress. She replied, "Honey, grits is like grace. It just comes."

These days, grace just comes. It's like a treasure hunt. Looking for glimpses of grace, signs of God's presence and provision for us, has become a habit. And I'm discovering grace every day:

- a good day for Steve
- a thoughtful clerk
- a surprise bargain
- a meaningful email
- words of encouragement
- a visit with an old friend
- small and big answers to prayer

These are reminders that I can only receive the day as it comes. And with it comes grace. Grace isn't something I can earn. I don't deserve it. It's pure gift.

Recently I've been chewing on Hebrews 4:16: "Let us therefore approach the throne of grace with boldness, so that we may receive mercy and find grace to help in time of need." We can come boldly to God's throne of grace because Jesus is there as our high priest, our advocate who understands our weakness and has experienced our temptations but never sinned. It's here that we receive mercy.

But we don't *receive* grace. We *find* it. Grace to help in time of need.

I'm reminded of the woman who found her lost coin, or the

shepherd who found the lost sheep or the father who found his runaway son. But first they searched. So I am searching for grace. And I'm finding it . . . every day.

Grace comes.

But sometimes you need to look for it.

Steve *October 31*

WHEN YOU CAN'T PLAN TOMORROW

Throughout my life I have been a planner and an activist. I have methodically kept a calendar of upcoming activities and carefully planned my days in order to get as much done as possible. I describe myself as an activist because I envision tasks and then set out to get them completed. I don't procrastinate and I generally finish tasks before deadlines. I work quickly. Some people see these qualities as virtues. I merely see them as personal characteristics, although they have certainly contributed to my ability to accomplish a lot of work in limited amounts of time.

While these qualities are still a part of my mindset, my cancer has landed me in a very unfamiliar place. These days, I can't reliably plan for tomorrow or next week. I don't know whether I will have the energy to accomplish what I would like to do. And my body is simply not physically dependable. Some days I feel good enough to conquer larger tasks, but I can never do any heavy lifting anymore. Some days I can endure work that takes longer than anticipated. Other days, my plans just have to fall by the wayside.

I've always counted it a privilege when I had periods of time with nothing at all planned—when what I did was entirely discretionary. But these were considered a gift and not the nature of my daily patterns. For the most part my daily schedules have been carefully shaped toward maximum productivity, whether that was relational or administrative.

So now I have to live with a lot of uncertainty. My body is not dependable. My energy level is not predictable. And even my mind frequently succumbs to what some call "chemo brain," when I am forgetful, unable to concentrate and lacking the ability to think things through as carefully as I once could.

I'm being forced to learn that when you can't plan tomorrow you have to develop new skills to seize today in whatever form it presents itself. Instead of putting tasks on the calendar, now I have to simply put them on a list of possibilities. When I assess how I am feeling on a particular day, I have to run through my list and do my planning on the fly.

I've lost a lot of efficiencies, but I am also gaining new skills in reflection and in more spontaneous activity. I'm realizing that keeping my schedule "full" is not the only healthy way to live, and that a slower and more thoughtful pace can be just as faithful. Listening to my body, listening for the Spirit and listening with an ear to the possibilities are important life skills too.

The apostle Paul's admonition to make "the most of every opportunity, because the days are evil" (Ephesians 5:16 NIV) takes on new meaning for me. It's not that the days are bad but rather that they can present us with wasted opportunities if we aren't prepared to seize the day and live into God's call.

LET ME GET HOME BEFORE DARK

As I write I am sitting in the recliner at the infusion center as the chemicals drip into my body. These are the hardest days for remembering that even in times of sickness I have a "call," even if it is limited to praying.

Robertson McQuilkin was a distinguished Bible school and college president for more than twenty years. But he may be best known for his early departure from office to care full-time for his wife, who battled Alzheimer's for decades. His powerful resignation speech and subsequent book (*A Promise Kept*) about what he learned from his sacrificial acts of love have encouraged countless people. You can catch some of the shape of Rev. McQuilkin's heart in this 1981 poem on the topic of contemplating death. The poem, sent to me by a friend, grabbed my attention again this week.

It's sundown, Lord.
The shadows of my life stretch back into the dimness of
years long spent.
I fear not death, for that grim foe betrays himself at last,
thrusting me forever into life, Life with you, unsoiled
and free.
But I do fear. I fear that Dark Specter may come too
soon—or do I mean, too late?
That I should end before I finish, or finish but not well.
That I should stain your honor, shame your name, grieve
your loving heart. Few, they tell me, finish well.
Lord, let me get home before dark.

The darkness of a spirit grown mean and small, fruit
shriveled on the vine, bitter to the taste of my
companions, burden to be borne by those brave few
who love me still.
No, Lord. Let the fruit grow lush and sweet, a joy to all
who taste; Spirit sign of God at work, stronger, fuller,
brighter at the end.
Lord, let me get home before dark.
The darkness of tattered gifts, rust-locked, half-spent or
ill-spent; A life that once was used of God now
set aside.
Grief for glories gone, or fretting for a task God never gave.
Mourning in the hollow chambers of memory,
Gazing on the faded banners of victories long gone. Cannot
I run well unto the end?
Lord, let me get home before dark.
The outer me decays. I do not fret or ask reprieve.
The ebbing strength but weans me from mother earth and
grows me up for heaven.
I do not cling to shadows cast by immortality.
I do not patch the scaffold lent to build the real, eternal me.
I do not clutch about me my cocoon, vainly struggling to
hold hostage a free spirit pressing to be born.
But will I reach the gate in lingering pain, body distorted,
grotesque?
Or will it be a mind wandering untethered among light
fantasies or grim terrors? Of your grace, Father, I
humbly ask . . .
Let me get home before dark.

CONTINUING THE JOURNEY OF FAITH

Over the last six months my life has completely changed. I currently feel pretty good and am able to carry on with a good schedule that includes time with people and projects. But I don't know how long any of this will last, and I seldom know from day to day how much I can plan to do. The only certainty that I have related to *this* world is that someday, sooner than I had planned, I will go home to be with Jesus.

Facing death has a way of clarifying life. So let me tell you a few things that I've learned in the last months.

1. When Jesus is all you have, you soon discover that Jesus is all you really need. One of the creeds of my denomination opens with the phrase, "In life and in death we belong to God." God created us . . . Jesus has redeemed us . . . and the Spirit transforms and gifts us for life every day. It is Christ who gives us meaning, purpose, worth and security. We look for these things in a variety of places: in our families, in our jobs, in our churches, in our convictions, in our health or wherever we think it can be found. But only in Jesus will we find Life with a capital *L*—abundant Life, which we experience now and which will last forever. *I'm in the process of losing everything that I have known on this earth, but I will never lose what God has given me in Christ.*

2. As long as I have life on this earth, I have a call. God has given me work to do and continues to give me work to do. Over my lifetime I have had many roles to play and many jobs to fulfill. But it is not the particulars of being a husband, a father, a grandfather, a friend, a seminary president, a World Vision board member or anything else that ultimately matters so much as the underlying call to be faithful. *God has called me to follow Jesus in everything I do*: to love the way Jesus loved, to listen to the Holy Spirit's promptings and to be obedient to God's commands. *Every day no matter how sick I become, I still have a call.*

3. God will never give up in his work to transform me into the likeness of Jesus. I fail every day at being and doing what God has intended. But God has promised to use everything in my life to continue the process of helping me to become more like Jesus in my thoughts, attitudes and behaviors. At this stage in my life God is using my disease to teach me. It's not easy and I don't like to change. But God loves me too much to give up on me. Therefore, *God uses my circumstances, whatever they are, to continue the process of transformation.*

4. Joy is not about my circumstances, but rather about being held and sustained by God's love. Nothing can ever separate us from the love of God—not suffering, not want, not abundance, not sin, not anything. God loves us from beginning to end and through every circumstance. *If there is one thing that I can trust, it is God's love for me in Christ Jesus.*

There is nothing new about any of these lessons. But God continues to remind me. And I continue to be grateful for every reminder.

On Halloween an unexpected reminder came from a trick-or-treater, who was about eight years old and was dressed like a little sheep. Surrounded by a flock of siblings, who were also dressed as sheep, he blurted out that they knew I was sick and were all praying for me.

"Thank you," I replied.

And then with big sincere eyes, he looked at me, smiled and said, "Heaven is going to be wonderful, you know?"

All I could think to say was, "It already is."

May God continue to bless, encourage, sustain and energize you for your call too. Who you are in Christ and what you are becoming really matters in *this* world—as well as the next.

Sharol *November 20*

HEALTH UPDATE: Chemo yesterday was a long process and not much fun, but thankfully this morning Steve has some energy and the ability to eat a full breakfast. We expect that he'll feel worse as the day progresses (how's that for positive thinking?) but are grateful for these early hours of grace. Yesterday, the doctor seemed very encouraged about Steve's health and the good days he has in each treatment cycle. The young doctor who works with the team asked where Steve got his positive attitude. Steve's face is full and his coloring is good—he looks healthy and quite robust. While I trudged up the four flights of stairs, Steve raced by me taking two steps at a time.

GRACE NOTES

I returned Tuesday from five days in California with my parents and sister. Steve encouraged me to go when we could find a window when he would feel well enough to be on his own. Even though I have nightly conversations on the phone with my mom, it was a gift to see her and my dad in person. Our days were full, seeing old friends and running errands. I was also able to spend time with Steve's sister who also lives in the Bay Area. Everywhere I went, people told me that they were praying for Steve and for me. It is a bit overwhelming but a picture of grace. We continue to feel surrounded by this great cloud of living witnesses who lift us to God and hold us up.

Steve had a wonderful few days here. He was able to spend two nights away from home with his good friends who pampered him and cared for him. Then Steve's brother came through Atlanta and stayed a couple of nights with Steve, something that doesn't happen that often. All in all, the days went quickly and Steve felt strong and able to be active all day. This too is a grace.

Our children and grandchildren will be here over Thanksgiving. With five grandchildren from eight years to six months, our time is bound to be full of laughter and abundant energy. It will truly be a memorable Thanksgiving when we again thank God for all his good gifts of grace. This year, we will be more thankful than ever

for life,
for time together,
for friends and family,
and for the wonders of living one day at a time.

Steve *November 26*

AM I WASTING MY TIME?

Recently I've been plagued by questions about how I am using my time. Knowing that my time on this earth is limited is a strong motivation to use the days I have left to the fullest. Some days, of course, I have little choice because I don't feel well enough to do much. There are natural, health-related limitations.

But on the days that I feel relatively good, I do have options. I look back some days and wonder whether I have been as faithful as I could be in how I have used my time.

- Have I accomplished enough?
- Should I have written more email messages or made more phone calls?
- Should I have been willing to see more people?
- Should I have worked on more projects that are on my list of possibilities?

I wonder some days how God regards my time. I'm sure that just being busy isn't the right criterion. Yesterday I was taking a little rest and found myself wondering whether resting was the right thing to be doing when I actually felt good enough to do more.

As I have said before, discerning and pursuing God's call for any particular day seems to be an important goal. But discernment isn't easy. Sometimes giving myself to little things, or simply to periods of thoughtful reflection, may be more important than my activist spirit will approve.

I find that I am developing internal questions to help me in my discernment. They include, for example:

- Is this activity something where my joy intersects with my perception of what brings joy to God?
- Am I living into this activity with gratitude for the opportunity given to me?
- Am I able to receive the time before me as a gift, or does it actually feel like a waste or a burden?

- Does this activity play into old patterns of procrastination on the one hand or overwork on the other?
- How does this activity express love—for God, for each other and for God's work in the world?

Woven into this whole process of discernment for me must be a clear perception of grace, otherwise all of this fuss does little more than encourage me to worry. If there is no joy in my life, then I am not listening to God's voice but only to my own perfectionism.

> *God makes a shocking statement in Ezekiel 16:14: "And your fame spread among the nations on account of your beauty, because the splendor I had given you made your beauty perfect, declares the Sovereign* LORD*" [*NIV*]. It strikes me that this is true of you, Steve, and of this time in your life. Living in and acting out his splendour will take a full-time commitment. Rest in his glory and enjoy him forever!*
>
> SARAH (ZIMMERMAN) MACINTOSH

I truly believe that "joy is the serious business of Heaven." C. S. Lewis made this important point in *Letters to Malcolm: Chiefly on Prayer*. Lewis pointed out that it is far too easy for us to assume that only the very serious things of life are approved by God. But in God's economy, where so much is upside down, even things that look frivolous, unimportant, wasteful or playful can be important when they are attached to the joy found in the heart of God's character.

So the real question about my day is not, "How productive was it?" but rather, "How much joy did my activity bring, and how much love and gratitude did it express?"

MORE WAITING

In the tradition of the Christian church, this is the season of Advent. It is a time when people prepare for Christmas by remembering the long wait between the many promises in the Old Testament and the coming of Jesus.

When I was first diagnosed with terminal cancer back in April, I didn't know if I would live to see another Christmas. Now it appears that I will, pending some unforeseen event. But waiting has taken on a new meaning for me. It's not about waiting for the next holiday, but rather about lingering in clinic waiting rooms or waiting for whatever event will signal that I am moving into another stage of my dying process.

Yesterday, for example, as I sat in the infusion chair with the chemotherapy dripping into my body, I had a terrible bout of "breakthrough pain," which I couldn't get under control for many hours. My pain has been fairly well controlled over these months, so this sort of thing is not typical and makes me wonder what will come next.

I'm actually not sure what will signal the next chapters. Perhaps it will be the point when my chemotherapy is no longer effective at managing the cancer and we will have to make the decision to end therapy. I have another diagnostic scan next Monday, so we should receive more information about what is actually happening with my cancer when we see the oncology team on the 17th. Perhaps the next chapter will be the time when my body noticeably begins to deteriorate again—when I begin losing weight, or when the pain begins to increase noticeably and regularly.

This final season of my life is all about waiting. It is not a waiting that I want to hurry along. But neither is it a waiting without hope. I am definitely not eager to die, nor am I eager to move into that stage of this process that includes more health challenges. But I also know that at the end of this waiting there will be peace of a sort that we cannot even imagine this side of eternity.

Waiting is a kind of tension and is hardly ever comfortable. We wait for friends, for phone calls, for medical reports and for bills to be paid. We wait for things to begin, and we wait for things to end. Some wait for a husband or a wife, or perhaps for a child. We wait for someone to notice us, or for someone to love us. We wait for reconciliation, for healing, for justice—for circumstances to change, and indeed for change in our own lives.

There is a pull between what is and what is to come. It is a tension that cannot be resolved. So instead, my choice is simply to watch with gratitude.

I am thankful for today and for all that comes with it. I try to be grateful, rather than impatient, in those waiting rooms. I am grateful for every day that I still have energy and the strength for more activity.

And I am thankful that there is a tomorrow that includes a glorious hope. In between, I am thankful for what I am learning and how I continue to grow.

For God alone my soul waits in silence;
from him comes my salvation.
He alone is my rock and my salvation,
my fortress; I shall never be shaken. (Psalm 62:1-2)

HEALTH UPDATE: It's been almost eight months since I was diagnosed with terminal pancreatic cancer. But apart from the days when I am recovering from the chemo treatments, I am still doing pretty well. I have various side effects from the chemo and cancer such as hair loss (I've got fuzz on my head again now), numbness in my feet and hands, digestive issues and loss of muscle tone. This week I've had what is referred to as "breakthrough pain" several times for which I have had to take extra medication. The cancer markers again elevated and have continued an upward trend for the past two months. Lately, I haven't felt as well and have slowed down. I just had another scan on Monday to see more clearly what is going on and will get a full report from the medical team next week.

LIVING IN LIGHT OF ETERNITY

The signals about my health are mixed. Some days we are encouraged and other days not so much.

Life can be confusing like this. We go through times that are encouraging and times that are discouraging. Often our feelings about what we are feeling are themselves confusing. Honestly, it's difficult to maintain a consistent perspective unless you are a person with an unusually stable personality.

When our children were teenagers and going through a stage where it seemed like every little thing took on immense proportions, I used to say to them, "So what do you think this is like in light of eternity?" In other words, is this really worth the fuss? But I have realized that it's not just kids who have a tough time with perspective. It's all of us.

We blow so many things out of proportion. Little things become huge issues. And even big things become issues that seem much bigger than they probably are. Whether it is a stressful circumstance, a difficult relationship, a confusing problem or a shameful failure, there is so much in our lives that feels like it will overwhelm us.

But the fact of the matter is that in light of eternity, most of what we face takes on a different proportion. Circumstances pass. Relationships can be healed. Even horrid failures are cut down to size by time and by God's grace at work in our lives.

Living with a life-threatening, terminal disease has a way of providing a different perspective. At least it can. Eternity is a little closer—a little more tangible. But I still feel confused from day to day about my situation. Am I really dying? How much longer can I expect to live? How do I stay encouraged when the evidence about my condition is mixed? What will the next stage of my disease be like? How do I live with consistency from day to day when my circumstances continue to vary?

What seems to be important now, as it has been throughout my illness, is that I keep my eyes on those things that remind me of eternity. There are loving relationships, for example, that call me back. And there is the centrality of joy, gratitude and service to be considered every day. All of these qualities keep my heart facing eternity rather than wallowing in inward confusion. It is the eternal focus that keeps me steady.

Love embraces me.

Joy uplifts me.

Gratitude settles me.

Service focuses me away from myself and back on the lives of others.

When I lean into love, joy, gratitude and service, I worry less, because eternity surrounds me and God's grace upholds me.

What does the inconsistency in my health mean in light of an eternity that is already assured? Ultimately day-to-day inconsistency means little when I live with my hand firmly held by the One who is the same yesterday, today and forever.

Steve *December 15*

I'M TIRED OF NOT FEELING WELL

I'm tired of not feeling well. I never know just how I will feel when I wake up in the morning, but I seldom feel really well anymore. There are always at least abdominal discomforts, neuropathy in my feet, miscellaneous little side effects from the cancer or chemo, and depression lurking in the corners.

This is the plight of those of us with chronic illness. It is giving me new empathy for the multitude of people who live with daily pain, depression, or disabling and degenerative diseases. So much of the time, there is nothing that can be done. It is what it is.

Sometimes time seems to drag along when I don't feel well. Other times, it goes far too quickly when I am coming up on another chemo treatment that I know is going to make me feel even worse.

But I don't want to be a complainer. I am committed to living into joy no matter what the circumstances.

So what helps?

- Focusing on an eternal perspective, which I have written about recently, certainly helps me to look outwardly rather than inwardly even when my body is screaming for my attention.

- Having a list of little projects, which give me something to look forward to and something to take my mind off my health.
- Distraction of all sorts helps. For example, I love having people around from time to time, as long as they are not too demanding. Sharol is terrific because some days she will just sit with me while I watch TV or read short pieces in a magazine (I am not able to focus well on reading anything long or complex).
- It helps me to take Saint Paul's advice when he writes (from his prison cell): "I'd say you'll do best by filling your minds and meditating on things true, noble, reputable, authentic, compelling, gracious—the best, not the worst; the beautiful, not the ugly; things to praise, not things to curse" (Philippians 4:8 *The Message*).

I am discovering that so much of living with chronic disease depends on my attitude. And my attitude requires that I be intentional. To what will I give my attention? What will I value? For what am I grateful?

Sharol *December 17*

HEALTH UPDATE: Today we met with Steve's oncologist to discuss the latest CT scan. Though Steve will have an abdominal CT scan on Monday to confirm his assumptions, the doctor believes that, based on evidence of growing cancer on the liver, Steve's pain in the area of the pancreatic tumor and his rising cancer markers, the chemo Steve has been on is no longer working and the cancer is spreading. Having already endured the five major pancreatic cancer–fighting drugs during two different chemotherapy regimens, Steve has opted to be put on the list for clinical drug trials. It could be six weeks before he would start a trial.

ALL KINDS OF MIRACLES

We are sad about the growing cancer, but we are not surprised. We both suspected that with increased pain and malaise, Steve's growing hair and diminishing neuropathy in his feet, something was going on and the chemo wasn't working.

So now we will focus on each day that we are given. Always, one day at a time. We are grateful for the eight months since Steve's diagnosis. He has outlived a huge percentage of fellow pancreatic cancer sufferers, and for that we are thankful. Of course, we hope for many more months ahead and for a miracle of physical healing. But we aren't without miracles during these past eight months.

Miracles of all kinds of healing.

Miracles of lives that have been impacted because of Steve's witness.

Miracles of peace and joy in the midst of difficult circumstances.

These are all answers to the prayers of so many.

Yesterday a friend reminded us of an Advent poem that Steve penned almost twenty-five years ago, a poem that I set to music. Steve wrote it on a napkin as we gathered with our small group in Madison, Wisconsin, and shared where we wanted to see God at work—those places in our lives where for years we had hoped we might experience transformation and healing. Mostly, in our helplessness that Advent, we could only say, "Come, Lord Jesus, come." This remains our prayer as we walk through the next days, weeks and months.

> *Thank you for continuing to take us behind the veil. The paradox of life and death remains a mystery to me, but not the power of the cross that helps us endure it. We love you both and sit with you in the uncertainty of the now, but not yet.*
>
> ED OLLIE JR

We are all terminal. We just happen to know it up close and personal. Our prayer for you and for us is "Come, Lord Jesus, come. We have prepared a place for you."

We will be gathering up our hopes and fears this next week as Jesus once again comes to our wooden manger in the fullness of time—between dinner and dessert on Christmas Eve. Missing from the manger for all of Advent, Jesus will come as the only one who can hold our hopes and our fears. We're ready to welcome him.

Advent

Is there grace enough to cover
The darkness I discover—
To light the inner places
Long cloaked in sad disgraces?
Come, Lord Jesus, come!

Is there love enough to lift me
When bold rebellion grips me
And failure bleakly presses
Guilt's overwhelming stresses?
Come, Lord Jesus, come!

Is there peace enough to hold me
When nagging fears erode me;
And strangling expectation
Turns hopes to desperation?
Come, Lord Jesus, come!

Is there joy enough to fill me
When barren reaches chill me
And grieving contemplation
Brings spirit's isolation?
Come, Lord Jesus, come!

Emilie Wagner *December 17*

HOPES AND FEARS OF ALL THE YEARS

"O Little Town of Bethlehem" . . . not one of my favorite Christmas carols, but when we sang it at church last week I was caught by this line: "The hopes and fears of all the years are met in thee tonight." I started thinking about this unbelievable promise that came with Jesus. This everlasting Light, fully human, fully God, came to redeem his people lost in darkness. Lost in their hopes and fears. Lost in themselves.

I understand the theology, but practically speaking I'm full of questions. How can this be? How are all my hopes and fears—the ones I can name, and the ones I haven't created yet, and the ones I forgot about long ago—how are they all met in Jesus?

So, I sat down to make a list of some of my hopes and fears. Some are big, some are small, but all feel significant in some piece of my heart. I quickly noticed that most of my fears are right on the other side of a hope, and vice versa. Here are a few from this week, in no particular order:

- I fear I'll forget the many details I'm juggling this week.
- I hope our kids will stay healthy so we can spend holidays with family.
- I fear that my dad, who has cancer, will have dark, painful days ahead.
- I fear that I won't adequately express my love and thanks for so many dear friends during this season. I hope I can focus outside myself even as I have so many things on my mind.
- I hope this stuff we keep teaching our kids about faith and love sticks with them. I fear that our mistakes will be stronger in their memory than the grace we try to extend.
- I hope I can be an agent of reconciliation as our community continues to wrestle with issues of race. I fear I'm not brave enough. I fear I have nothing meaningful to add to the conversation.

With some of these, just speaking them aloud gave me space to see where Jesus is already at work. For instance, I know Jesus loves our children even more than I do, and that there is incredible grace as we parent. But others loom large in my mind. Can it be true that Jesus is who he says he is even in that?

I am approaching the manger this Christmas with my hopes and fears in hand, with faith that Jesus is indeed the "Wonderful Counselor, Mighty God, Everlasting Father, Prince of Peace. Of the increase of his government and of peace there will be no end" (Isaiah 9:6-7 ESV). It's an impossible promise you can count on.

MY LAST CHRISTMAS

It's Christmas morning—likely the last time my family and I will spend this celebration together. I feel a certain responsibility to make it memorable, or to somehow do it right. But I'm not sure what that means. And I'm not off to a very good start. Yesterday I tried. And I practically ruined the day, at least for myself.

Christmas Eve is a big day of traditions in our home, and the family was all gathered. But, instead of just enjoying the day, I found myself getting grumpy about the little things that went wrong. The grandkids were frequently unable to get along. One of our kids had a stomach virus and couldn't participate. The schedule kept changing. And I kept feeling that I was the only one who really cared about making this a really good day. So instead of delighting in the family and in the activities, I found myself muttering under my breath—as unhappy with myself as I was with everyone else.

Yet despite my bad attitude, it was a pretty good day. The children had a lot of fun. Our traditional birthday party for Jesus in the evening was festive and meaningful. Our wooden nativity scene, which has not included the baby Jesus throughout Advent, secretly received the baby Jesus between dinner and dessert as it does every year. We had our usual ice cream cake. And after dessert we all enjoyed the family Christmas pageant.

This year the highlight for me was watching our eight-month-old grandson dressed up like a sheep crawling around between the legs of Joseph and two Marys (we have two granddaughters who both wanted to be Mary).

I'm glad that my grumpy Christmas Eve is over and that it is now Christmas morning. I'm hoping I can let go today. Surely doing today better means relaxing into whatever happens and giving up my need to make it perfect. Surely having a great time together includes being authentic and transparent in our relationships with one another. And I'm pretty sure that for me it means shedding some tears of both joy and grief.

Thank you for your words on the joy and mystery of Christ's glorious birth. So much you have shared from the valley of the shadow of death brings light and hope to all of us. I just returned from the hospital to see our congregation's Christmas Eve baby. Thinking of you, and your life, and thinking of God's gift of life in the birth of a child. Praise God, for as proclaimed in Romans 14, "If we live, we live to the Lord, and if we die, we die to the Lord; so then, whether we live or whether we die, we are the Lord's."

W. MARK GEORGE

Mary, the mother of Jesus, was certainly not in control of that first Christmas. But her response was much better than mine as she "treasured all these words and pondered them in her heart" (Luke 2:19).

Phillips Brooks's words (from "O Little Town of Bethlehem") are a helpful reminder:

How silently, how silently, the wondrous gift is given,
So God imparts to human hearts the blessings of his heaven.
No ear may hear his coming, but in this world of sin
Where meek souls will receive him still, the dear Christ enters in.

God's greatest gift came into the world quietly, and unpretentiously. Were it not for the wild chorus of angels announcing the birth to a few shepherds on a hillside, this momentous occasion might have gone unnoticed altogether that night. Today I want to be one of the "meek" ones—one of the humble, attentive, yielding lambs into whose life God can quietly enter, bringing whatever joy is a part of today.

Steve *January 1*

HEALTH UPDATE: This week we said goodbye to the medical oncology team who have taken good care of me for the past eight months. The final tests confirmed that there is nothing more that can be done for my case at the Emory Winship Cancer Institute. This is not a surprise. There are new tumors throughout my liver, and the tumor on the head of my pancreas has almost doubled in size. There was the possibility that I could go into a phase-one clinical trial, but the big question for me was how I wanted to spend my last months. A drug trial guarantees nothing and, optimistically, could only give me an extra month or two of life if it were effective. In exchange for this, I would have to be committed to more medical tests and procedures, chemotherapy of some sort, and a range of possible side effects. We decided that there are better ways that we would like to spend these last months.

NEW YEAR, LAST CHAPTER

I remain committed to the conviction that every day still contains both a call from God and a journey from which I need to learn.

So with this New Year comes a new chapter. *I am now offi-*

cially under hospice care. This new team will walk me to the finish line of this life. I will have whatever medical, social and spiritual support I need from both the hospice team and our family, friends, church and seminary families.

Facing the hard realities of this new chapter is not easy. Sharol and I are grieving. Even when we have known for months that I only had a short time to live, we have had only had a vague timeline. But being in hospice makes it more concrete. The lists that I have been working with in my head are now receiving deadlines for completion. For example, we pray more fervently to be able to complete the renovation of our house so that we can get all moved in before my last days.

I am so thankful for a family with whom we can have the conversations that could feel so awkward. One of the hospice admission people asked Sharol whether I knew what hospice meant, because apparently many families don't even tell the person who is dying what the realities are.

For us the most difficult part of this latest transition has been the uncertainties of what would happen next. What has been so relieving is how easy it actually has been so far. The social worker at the cancer institute handled all of the initial steps of moving me into hospice care, including contacting the

> *We have all known this was a mortal struggle you were in. You have shown us how to fight the good fight, never alone, always trusting that you were not in control of the outcome. But now that we hear that outcome, it is hard, hard. All of us would have hoped for another. In grief, but with gratitude to you and Sharol for being our mentors in faith, and sharing so very honestly, and deeply, your struggles and quiet triumphs.*
>
> GRETA REED

hospice organization that we have chosen and making sure that all medical records got into the right hands. The hospice people are providing all the support that we need for what is typically the last six months of life. They are available to us twenty-four hours a day as needed, will take care of all my medications and will scale their services to exactly what we need as the time goes on and my condition changes.

Today, I'm just relaxing into the gratitude of having such good care.

Today, I'm not afraid, though some fears will undoubtedly sneak up on me as I get sicker.

Today, I'm trying to be attentive to what is happening to me without feeling like I have to be responsible for everything.

Today, I am living once again into joy.

Sharol *January 8*

CAREGIVING

Being a caregiver is hard work. Currently, I can handle the physical aspects of caregiving as Steve is still quite self-sufficient. It's a matter of patience and a willingness to be a servant—not always my first reaction, but I've been surprised that serving has been easier than I imagined. Having said this, I'll probably struggle tomorrow with a good attitude, but most days, I find it a privilege to serve Steve.

The difficult part is the emotional aspect of caregiving. Though I hate to watch Steve suffer, as long as we know how to handle what is happening in his body, I sleep well at night and don't worry. But several weeks ago as Steve reacted strongly to the chemo drugs and the antinausea meds weren't doing their job, my stomach was in a jumble right along with his. I was awake for several hours one night wondering if I should call the cancer center. Did he throw up his meds? Was he becoming dehydrated? Was I ready to be without him? These questions, highlighting my helplessness and powerlessness, loomed larger than reality in the darkness of night.

This is why beginning the journey with hospice brings amazing relief. Someone else now takes responsibility for Steve's meds. Someone with training in end-of-life issues is watching over his care. When we arrived home after making the decision to enroll in hospice, Steve confessed that he felt strangely encouraged. I, too, was encouraged.

We feel deep peace over this decision even though the reality of Steve's death stares us in the face.

You don't talk about hospice without talking about dying. But somehow in the conversations we've had with each other, with our family and with various ones who are now part of Steve's support team, talking of death isn't scary or dark or overwhelming.

In my younger years, I would have avoided these conversations. But now, having walked this shadowed path with friends and now with Steve for almost nine months, I see these conversations as sacred.

These are holy conversations where the Spirit of God is very present. This is a sacred journey where the distance between heaven and earth shrinks. The moments we share are holy moments, brushes with eternity. A place of peace, of shalom. A place of gratitude. I am so thankful.

WHAT TIME IS IT?

For everything there is a season, and a time for every matter under heaven:
a time to be born, and a time to die. (Ecclesiastes 3:1-2)

I've been pondering recently what time it is—this time of waiting, of watching, of wondering as we walk with Steve through the remaining weeks of his life.

It's a time for being peacefully present alongside Steve, whose mind and body are slowing down as the cancer grows. I'm aware that this is a calling. I pray to be faithful.

It's a time for laughter and for tears. We laughed a lot with our children and grandchildren and good friend Tim Dearborn this past weekend even as we shed many tears, tears that come easily and unexpectedly.

It's a time for saying yes to speaking truthfully in potentially difficult conversations; yes to kind offers of help and food; yes to friends who are walking with us through thick and thin. Today we talked about postponing our move from the president's house at Columbia Seminary to our house here in Decatur. I have been sensing in the past week that this move could be disruptive for Steve and quite distracting for me. We agreed this morning that we will stay here for these weeks, grateful for the seminary's hospitality.

It's a time for saying no to things that are not life giving. There's not enough time to act out of obligation or merely to please others. I often say no to the very things that might bring relief and yes to the things that distract and get in the way. How easy it is to mix these up.

It's a time for saying no to some life-giving things as well. I find it difficult not to respond to the notes and expressions of love that many of you have sent. But I don't have the energy. One day I might, but for now I must give myself permission to say no.

This is a time for gentleness—gentleness with each other and with ourselves, gentleness when our brokenness keeps popping up. It's a time to live in grace—the all-sufficient grace of Jesus Christ that God promises when we are weak and vulnerable.

It's a time for gratitude. Even in the worst of times, there is always something for which to be thankful. Today I'm thankful for an amazing hospice doctor who comes and sits with us and explains what's going on physically for Steve but also asks questions about our emotional and spiritual journeys. I'm grateful for emails and texts from so many who have felt nudged to pray for us. This is a rich reminder to me that we are not alone and that the Spirit continues to be at work. I would never have guessed that this process of death and dying would be life giving not only for us but also for many of you as we stand together on holy ground and peek around the corner at the future God has laid out for us.

What time is it? It's a time for grief but it's also a time for gratitude. As one friend says, grief and gratitude mixed together create joy. How true this is.

IT'S NOT ABOUT DOING IT RIGHT

On Tuesday night, Steve's condition suddenly worsened so that the hospice doctor encouraged me to call our grown children to come to Steve's bedside—that his death was probably imminent. So they came late that night, Emilie and her husband, Chad, and Drew and his girlfriend, Stephanie. Because it was so late, Chip decided to drive down from Nashville the next morning, fully expecting that Steve would be gone by the time he arrived.

That night, we cried and said our goodbyes. We sat on our bed and held Steve's hands and prayed and laughed some. In the meantime, several dear friends from far and near gathered in the living room to tell stories about Steve and pray and sing and keep vigil. It was an amazing night of sadness and joy.

Steve awakened Wednesday morning, alive and alert and able to talk. As the CTS community gathered that day in the chapel to pray for Steve and the family, to read Scripture and poetry and to sing, Steve, ever alert, sent his greetings to the seminary community. The CTS communications director posted on Facebook that the official word at Columbia Seminary was that Steve was in transition. The unofficial word was that Steve was sending text messages!

Yesterday and this morning, Steve continues to be alert and communicative though very weak. We have continued to sit with him, saying our goodbyes, telling stories, laughing, crying. Wondering at his ability to live when he has had nothing to eat or drink except ice chips. Grateful for the hospice doctor who continues to be attentive to Steve, keeping his pain and nausea under control. Thankful for a community of friends who have graciously been present downstairs, offering food, prayers, stories and encouragement throughout the week. It has been a precious, unforgettable time.

> *When the moment comes and the catcher catches, I pray that some glory may leak back to all of you holding vigil. May the sharp edges of your being left here be softened by bearing witness to glory.*
>
> KEVIN FORD

Steve is so ready to die and we have released him to do so, but as he said this morning, he just can't make it happen.

A friend shared this excerpt from theologian and writer Henri Nouwen. We just read it to Steve and it resonated with him.

> The Flying Rodleighs are trapeze artists who perform in the German circus Simoneit-Barum. When the circus came to Freiburg two years ago, my friends Franz and Reny invited me and my father to see the show. I will never forget how enraptured I became when I first saw the Rodleighs move through the air, flying and catching as elegant dancers. The next day, I returned to the circus to see them again and introduced myself to them as one of their great fans. They invited me to attend their practice sessions, gave me free tickets, asked me to dinner, and suggested I travel with them for a week in the near future. I did, and we became good friends.
>
> One day, I was sitting with Rodleigh, the leader of the troupe, in his caravan, talking about flying. He said, "As a flyer, I must have complete trust in my catcher. The public

might think that I am the great star of the trapeze, but the real star is Joe, my catcher. He has to be there for me with split-second precision and grab me out of the air as I come to him in the long jump." "How does it work?" I asked. "The secret," Rodleigh said, "is that the flyer does nothing and the catcher does everything. When I fly to Joe, I have simply to stretch out my arms and hands and wait for him to catch me and pull me safely over the apron behind the catch bar."

"You do nothing!" I said, surprised. "Nothing," Rodleigh repeated. "The worst thing the flyer can do is to try to catch the catcher. I am not supposed to catch Joe. It's Joe's task to catch me. If I grabbed Joe's wrists, I might break them, or he might break mine, and that would be the end for both of us. A flyer must fly, and a catcher must catch, and the flyer must trust, with outstretched arms, that his catcher will be there for him."

When Rodleigh said this with so much conviction, the words of Jesus flashed through my mind: "Father into your hands I commend my Spirit." Dying is trusting in the catcher. To care for the dying is to say, "Don't be afraid. Remember that you are the beloved child of God. He will be there when you make your long jump. Don't try to grab him; he will grab you. Just stretch out your arms and hands and trust, trust, trust."

FULLNESS OF JOY

Steve's life was swallowed up by *Life* this afternoon. As we had prayed, and he had written about, he went home "before dark," without pain and surrounded by family and dear friends.

We are grieving, but not as those who have no hope. Truly, it was beautiful to walk him home together, and we trust that he is now experiencing the fullness of joy in Jesus' presence.

Steve Harrington, who has been a friend of ours for three decades, recently wrote about a memory of a time together with Steve on a retreat. He has turned the memory into a parable that speaks deeply to me every time I read it:

> My favorite unique memory with you was years ago at Wellspring Retreat Center. You remember we were given various iterations of the "trust walk." In one of those exercises we were supposed to guide our blindfolded partner from behind using only our voice. You walked in front of me and I directed you with only words into a small thicket of woods. I had you stepping over logs and ducking down below strong branches. You went slowly and could feel dead wood snapping beneath your feet and all of the twigs on your face as you brushed past them. You knew that you were walking through a very thick and tangled terrain—a precarious path for someone blindfolded and having to trust only the words spoken to them.
>
> Then I brought you almost out of the woods to the very edge of a large flat grassy field and stopped you six inches from the grass—you were still standing in the woods blind-

folded (you remember, right?). You had no idea that all the tangles and tripping hazards and undergrowth and slapping branches and hard trees were behind you and that before you was only a broad, flat, lush field of green grass. You were still in the woods imagining yourself stuck in the midst of all the tangles and hazards. Only I knew that before you it was all level and open and free of any encumbrance or danger or fear.

Then I said, at the count of three I want you to run straightforward as fast as you can.

I counted to three and, with great trust, you took off running, charging ahead, screaming your lungs out, flailing your arms—worried that you were still careening through the woods but also suddenly laughing to find out that you were out of the tangled danger and running easily into a flat field full of soft and forgiving grass.

This is the journey ahead for you my friend, whenever it is that you take it. The Word is behind you but also goes before you; the Word made flesh walks with you and is within you. And therefore all shall be well, and all shall be well—and all manner of things shall be well. The nausea and the discomfort, the fear and weakness, the tears and the treatments (the tripping hazards and the threatening thicket) will be over and you will run full speed screaming and laughing into the forgiving arms of grace and the healing heart of God.

Steve is in God's forgiving arms of grace and the healing heart of God.

I pray that this parable will be an encouragement to you too—whatever you are facing.

JOY . . . FULLY

Ours was not a perfect marriage. There were so many times when we gave each other the remnants of our day. The joy that some have written about was often down to the last drop. There were many ragged edges. But ours was definitely a "good enough" marriage. Our foundation was strong and the past nine months only made it stronger. Wonderfully and mercifully, our 24/7 relationship in the past months was a sweet gift.

I am a mixture of tears and gratitude these days. I miss Steve so much and think of him off and on all day. I momentarily forget he is not here—wanting to tell him something or forward him an email. Many times a day I think, "Steve, you would love this!" So I've begun to ask Jesus to pass on my messages to Steve, grateful that in his perfected state, Steve will always listen and will smile that radiant smile.

Psalm 16 was a favorite of ours.

Protect me, O God, for in you I take refuge.
I say to the LORD, *"You are my Lord;*
I have no good apart from you."
As for the holy ones in the land, they are the noble,
in whom is all my delight.
Those who choose another god multiply their sorrows;
their drink offerings of blood I will not pour out
or take their names upon my lips.
The LORD *is my chosen portion and my cup;*
you hold my lot.

The boundary lines have fallen for me in pleasant places;
I have a goodly heritage.
I bless the Lord *who gives me counsel;*
in the night also my heart instructs me.
I keep the Lord *always before me;*
because he is at my right hand, I shall not be moved.
Therefore my heart is glad, and my soul rejoices;
my body also rests secure.
For you do not give me up to Sheol,
or let your faithful one see the Pit.
You show me the path of life.
In your presence there is fullness of joy;
in your right hand are pleasures forevermore.

When Steve was interviewing for his first call at University Presbyterian Church in Seattle, the committee thoughtfully brought us both, still engaged, to the interview. Psalm 16 became our companion. The lines had indeed "fallen for us in pleasant places"; we had a "goodly heritage." Nurturing and loving families, mentors who called out our gifts, friends who faithfully journeyed with us.

We dared to believe that the Lord truly was at our right hand and that indeed through the work of the Spirit our hearts would instruct us in the night as we discerned God's call, not just for Steve but for me as well. We welcomed the Lord's presence, made real to us in Jesus, where we would find fullness of joy.

Psalm 16 has fortified and instructed us all through our forty-two years of life together, but I have a fresh understanding of the last verse in the psalm. Steve is now face-to-face with God, fully in God's presence, and he is knowing fullness of joy. No more scarcity, no more mere drops, but abundant, overflowing fullness.

Joy . . . fully.

When we pray "thy kingdom come on earth as it is in heaven," that prayer is being answered as we celebrate the many ways that God used Steve to help us take steps toward Jesus and toward the things that Jesus loves—new life, justice, reconciliation, peace, forgiveness, joy. My heart is full even in grief.

Emilie Wagner *February 11*

THE MINISTRY OF "BEING WITH"

"You need to come," my mom said. "The doctor says you need to come." My dad had been in hospice care since New Year's Eve, so this phone call two weeks ago wasn't a surprise to me. Still, I bent over in tears. Anticipating an event isn't the same as walking through it.

Our dear friends came to stay with our kids, who were tucked in for the night, and my husband and I drove the familiar road to my parents' house. It was a faster, slower trip than any I could remember. I was scared Papa would die before we arrived. I was scared he wouldn't, and that I'd be there when he did. So many emotions, most of which I couldn't name.

Relief overcame my anxiety when we arrived to find six cars parked out front. The lights inside were warm. Through the windows I could see friends gathered—some I'd known from childhood, some I had met recently, a doctor from hospice who I knew was a friend even though we had not yet met. Because they were there, the path to the house was dark but safe.

That was a Tuesday. Papa surprised us all and lived until Saturday, lucid and full of laughter until the very end. And the friends didn't leave. Through the days and nights, these friends brought coffee, shared meals, told stories, laughed a lot and sat quietly.

I still can't describe exactly why this was important. Beyond the logistics of keeping our family fed and rested, there wasn't a lot for these friends to do. There was clearly nothing to fix or accomplish as we waited for Papa to die. But there was a gift in

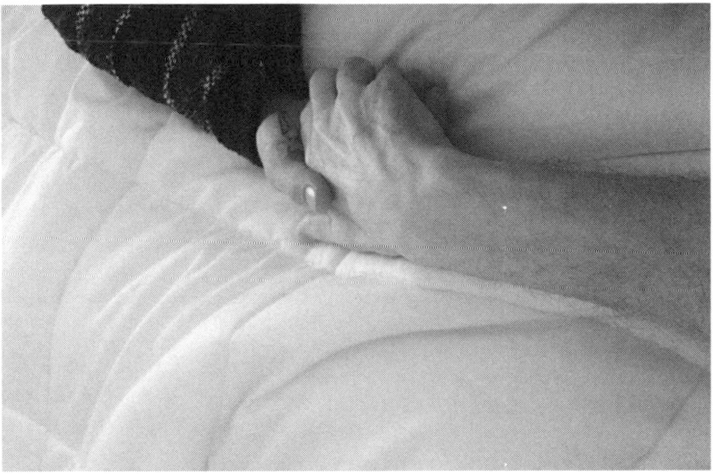

Steve and his son Drew holding hands. Photo by Emilie Warner.

being together—a gift that some call the "ministry of presence," the ministry of "being with."

This ministry of "being with" is a reflection of God's heart for us. We see this clearly in God's gift of Jesus, whom he called Emmanuel, "God with us." God also sent his Spirit to be with us always. It is because of his great love for us that God wants to be with us, and designed us to be with one another.

Had our family been alone during those days, I wonder if the stench of death would have overwhelmed the joy of life for a time. Something about "being with" made us able to see both life and death—the beautiful terrible—together.

We weren't made for death, but we can grieve as people who hope in God's forever love (1 Thessalonians 4:13).

Together, we trust God's great promise of a new heaven and a new earth where, as we read in Revelation 21:3-4, "The dwelling place of God is with man. He will dwell with them, and they will be his people, and God himself will be with them as their God. He will wipe away every tear from their eyes, and death shall be no more, neither shall there be mourning, nor crying, nor pain anymore, for the former things have passed away" (ESV).

Thanks be to God.

Sharol *February 18*

SUCH STRANGE SORROW

It's hard to believe that it's been two and a half weeks since Steve died. I have experienced a mix of deep sadness and great joy and everything in between. There are hours when I am caught up in normal life with decisions to be made,

Those of us far away who couldn't be there (you would have needed a stadium if all had come who wanted to be there!) are grateful for the care you and your three children took to include us through the power of the Internet. All this is a foretaste of the ultimate Ministry of Presence we will one day join Steve in celebrating, as we live forever in the presence of the Father, Son and Holy Spirit . . . lost in wonder, love and praise.

TIM TEUSINK

legal issues to attend to, people to love, guests to welcome. It is easy to laugh and leave behind the events of these last months. Then, with little warning, I am overwhelmed with a memory of Steve, and the tears flow.

Missionary Ken Old wrote of his sorrow when his wife, Marie, died:

Grieving is such strange sorrow!
A calm and quiet sea of thankfulness
Broken, unexpected, unawares
By a wave from deep below,
Splashing only tears.

Sharol *February 28*

GRIEF, GRATITUDE AND JOY

Now that Steve's memorial service is over and I resume a more normal routine, I am reminded that there is nothing normal about my life. I'm used to being independent, but Steve was always coming home from somewhere or calling from somewhere or at his desk at home. I miss his presence, his laugh, his wisdom, his joy. But I am profoundly grateful for the many years we shared together and for his life. I was and am so much more because of him. Together we have three—really five, including their spouses—amazing children and five very special grandchildren who encourage, love and bring much joy to me. God is faithful.

Steve would close by reminding us all to live one day at a time before an audience of One, trusting in God who loves us so much and for whom there are no dead ends. He would remind us that no matter our circumstances, God has a call for us. And that as we remember whose we are and live faithfully as ladies and gentlemen—honoring and encouraging one another—and as scholars—not only of people and culture but of the Word, and most importantly of Jesus—God will be at work in us, making what we do last and bringing about God's kingdom on earth.

Now to the One who is able to do exceedingly abundantly beyond all we could ask or even imagine according to his power at work in us, to God be the glory in the church and in Christ Jesus both now and forever more. (Ephesians 3:20-21, paraphrase).

And all God's people said, *Amen.*

Epilogue

Journeying to Final Joy

The following comments are adapted from the tributes that were given at Steve's memorial service on February 23, 2015.

READY FOR HEAVEN: TIM DEARBORN

In Steve's last weeks, Steve and Sharol's journey demonstrated something many would say we've rarely witnessed. In fact, their hospice doctor, who herself is a graduate of Columbia Seminary, suggested that Steve and Sharol are rewriting the chapter for pastoral theology textbooks on the journey toward death. The hospitality that characterized the Hayners' living, they extended even to Steve's dying.

We were deeply moved to see that rather than fleeing, resisting or denying the approaching reality, they expressed both lament and trust. They held together deep grief over this mysterious, and from our perspective, premature passing—while resolutely affirming their faith in the steadfast love of God.

Steve was ready to die, and in his last days when he awoke each morning still here, he expressed a degree of surprise and even disappointment.

Always eager for advice and counsel from Steve, when I spent the weekend with the Hayner family the week before Steve died, I asked him if he had any words of advice for us. Though lying weakly on his bed, dulled slightly by pain and morphine, Steve was stunningly bright, positive and insightful. When I asked what he was learning about dying, he said,

> Not knowing what's coming in the next weeks is the hardest part. It's hard to wait for death knowing it is coming through a gradual shutting down of bodily and mental functioning. But it does give me the opportunity to live it with acceptance, joy and brightness. I feel shame about declining physically and about needing morphine, and it's humiliating to have others remind me to take pills. Yet there's a deep sense of the importance of camaraderie with those who are willing to live it with me. So I don't have to live it with shame but just live it.

Knowing he was unlikely to offer any advice, since that wasn't his style, I prodded him. "Come on, Steve, this is our last chance. What advice do you have for us?" He replied,

> Life is a whole lot less complicated and a whole lot more joyful than I'd ever imagined. The grace and love of God permeate more of life than we dare to realize. Often I've taken life and myself way too seriously, and God never meant life to be lived that way. It's meant to be lived with joy and playfulness. The outcome is good and terrific. I wish I'd played more. But now I'll have lots of opportunity to grow into that. As C. S. Lewis says, "Joy is the serious business of Heaven."

I added, "And heaven is more like our play than our work."

Steve had a deep determination to sign everything "joyfully." Now he is enjoying the serious work of heaven. His life is signed with joy. I believe he is praying that we'll all practice it a little more fully with one another here, now.

ON LEAVING A LEGACY: CHIP HAYNER

Over his lifetime, my dad gave advice to countless people. As his son, I'm no different. I got advice about what kind of water heater to get when mine broke (I got a tankless, and it was amazing). I got advice about how to choose the right Christmas tree (you must always get a Fraser Fir, preferably one you can cut down yourself). I got advice about not setting my cruise control more than 10 percent over the speed limit (although I regrettably wish I had better listened to that one).

Papa articulated some of his best advice to me, however, in his last few days as I sat with him on his bed. Despite his weaker condition, he turned to me and with conviction said, "Don't worry about leaving a legacy. Just worry about being faithful . . . and God will do the rest."

The words stuck from the moment they came out of his mouth, and they will stick with me forever. They are the core of who he is.

Papa lived this advice in his own life. Rarely, if ever, did I hear him talk about his public reputation, his influence among the Christian community or his unimaginable network that allows you to easily play "Six Degrees of Steve Hayner." Instead, I heard him talking about all of the great things that the organizations he served were doing; the amazing trips he took to visit the poor, the needy and the oppressed; the individuals with whom he served and led. This was his focus in his day-to-day life—not striving to "leave a legacy."

For me these words really are a culmination of what he has been teaching me my whole life.

BECAUSE HE WAS MY PAPA: EMILIE WAGNER

I loved Papa very much—I still do. He was my dad—our dad.

I've been asked countless times in the past few weeks, "Aren't you proud of your dad?" "I read that article about him—I saw all those Facebook posts—you must be so proud of your Papa!"

I've been struggling with how to respond to this question because, quite frankly, it's not something I had thought much about until recently. I admired his passion for justice. I appreciated his wisdom. I loved his laugh. But I don't know if I would have said I was proud of him most of my life because, well, he was just my dad.

My brothers and I rarely saw him in the roles of teacher or preacher. We didn't know him as pastor or president or board member. He was just our dad—the one who walked super fast on vacation and who thought the food court at the mall was fancy dining. He was our Papa who talked *really* loudly on the phone, and who lamented that his move to the warmer climate of Georgia meant he could no longer wear his favorite sweaters. To us he was that goofy guy who did ridiculous dances, showing what was recently described as "dorky joy."

I loved all of these things about him. But did they make me proud? In a way I guess they did, in the same way that I'm proud of my kids every day, no matter what. I was proud of him because he was mine. We were all proud of him for that. He was our Papa.

But you know, in his last months, I saw some things in Papa that made me—made all of us—really proud. We watched as sickness softened his heart, when it could have grown cold instead. Weakened by the cancer in those last weeks, he was more tenderhearted and quietly reflective than I had ever experienced, and funnier too. I was very proud of that man who continued to share blessing with family and friends in his last days on earth.

The day before Papa died, he and I sat on his bed, much as we had all been doing throughout the week. With his eyes closed, he reflected on his years of preaching about God's love that never gives up—God's love that comes to those who don't deserve it, no matter who we are or what we've done.

"You know the truth, though?" Papa said to me. "I've never been able to *really* believe it for myself. My whole life I've doubted that God could really love me."

I was so proud of him in that moment.

See, I have doubts about myself that don't fit with the beauty and truth I can see in others. You probably do too. What bravery Papa had to say it out loud, trusting that his doubt didn't make his faith any less real.

I'm proud of Papa because he was just a guy, our dad, who knew in the end that his accomplishments were nothing compared to Jesus. He loved us the best he knew how, and for the rest he trusted that God was bigger. Papa trusted that he belonged to Jesus—that he was a small piece of something more.

Thanks be to God for his life on earth and his new life with *his* Papa in heaven, where he is now sure that he is fully loved.

God with Us

A Confession of Faith

Stephen A. Hayner

When God created the heavens and the earth
When God created all that lives
He crowned creation with humankind
And said, "This is very good."
The people who walked in Light,
Walked in perfect fellowship with God;
In perfect harmony with each other and with the earth.
They were whole, alive, full of joy, without fear;
They knew who they were because they knew whose they were.
But they grew proud in their sufficiency,
In their abundance they forgot God.
They turned within themselves for answers
And the Light flickered out.
The people of the Light became the people of darkness.
Once they were God's people—now they were no people.
Over the years many proposed that the darkness was normal.
Others tried to dispel the darkness with small glimmerings.
Still others, too proud to admit that something was wrong,
Just pretended that they didn't notice.

But in the darkness lurked the fears, the sins, the insecurities,
the hurts, the sufferings, the guilt, the loneliness,
and ultimately the death which no one could finally avoid.
The Good News—God's News—is that he never gave up.
The Author of Light was not content for a moment to watch
His good and perfect creation
Spin worthlessly off toward eternal darkness—
Infinite separation from himself.
So he began to work out his plan.
He sought out people in the darkness who in faith
Would live by the Light which they could not see.
Then, when the time had fully come, God sent his Son.
What the people living in the darkness could never do
God did by sending the One-who-was-Light into the dark.
This Light, this Life, this Lord shone in the darkness
But the darkness could not comprehend.
He came to the world which by virtue of creation belonged
to him,
But the world did not recognize him or embrace him.
Yet to all who received him, he gave the right to become children
of God—
Not because they were good,
Not because they tried hard to please,
Not because they were worthy in any way,

But because in his love, God never gives up.
Few welcomed him at his coming;
He slipped into the world so quietly.
He might have come completely unnoticed had God not been
overcome
By his own joy.
To some shepherds who were not accustomed to receiving mail,
God sent a birth announcement
On the wings and songs of a million angels.
He sent another written in the stars to some Gentile astrologers.
While he lived among us, not many believed in him.
There were a few fishermen, who were not really looking for a
new job;
A couple of tax collectors, who probably should have been
looking for a new job;
And a few handicapped folks who had been wishing for years
that they could get a job.
He called each of them by name.
He brought Light into their darkness;
Wholeness into their lives;
Eternity into their souls.
Jesus Christ who was Light, so threatened the darkness that
humankind did what they had been doing to God for years—
They tried to box him up,

They sentimentalized him,
They tried to explain him away,
And finally they killed him.
But God raised him from the dead.
The Light would never again go out.
The Holy Spirit was sent to burn within those who believed in him.
Ablaze, the no people again became God's people.
He still brings Light.
As quietly as he slipped into the world,
He now slips into believing hearts—
As surely as he changed the world by his coming,
No person remains the same after meeting the living Christ.
This is the Good News.

Acknowledgments

This book came about because of a call to travel a road we had neither considered nor chosen. The gift was the travelers who accompanied us. Our children, Emilie and her husband, Chad Wagner, Chip and his wife, Kristen, and Drew, along with our grandchildren, Claire, Anna, David, Lainey and Jack, became part of our story as we wandered through the hills and valleys of pancreatic cancer. I will never forget our gathering in July when Steve's MRI showed that the first chemotherapy regimen was not working. Steve and I wanted to share firsthand this news with our kids, news that they courageously and tearfully received. It was on that day that the "happiest family on earth" pictures were taken. A lovely contrast to our weeping several hours earlier. Our journey has been like that—hilarious laughter and deep sorrow.

Mary Banks and Stuart Knechtle have been our guides from the very beginning. They were God's gift to us, along with Doug and Jean Taylor and Maggie, Fiona and Logan who as next-door neighbors and long-time friends brought food and love and needed help. Who would have imagined when we all lived in Madison, Wisconsin, that we would end up in Atlanta within two miles of each other? For such a time as this.

Our many friends from far and near and our family scattered around the country have faithfully prayed for us, sent encouraging notes, traveled to spend precious time with us and arrived at just the right moment. A special thank you to all who felt the nudge to come, sometimes at the last minute like Mark Labberton and Thomas Daniel who on the day before Steve died shared communion with us and those at our house, representing their wives, Janet and Beth, and a host of loved ones who could not be there. Cherished memories.

Thank you to Columbia Seminary faculty, staff and students who lovingly brought food, notes, communion, encouragement and prayers, all reminders that relationships are not about position and capabilities but about grace, love and mercy. I am indebted to Bill Scheu, Deb Mullen and Marty Sadler who with the board of trustees graciously let us stay in the president's house and helped us navigate the many decisions around Steve's disability. They came alongside us in ways that were abundantly generous and so appreciated.

Our thanks go to our Kairos Church family in Atlanta who in so many ways exhibited the love of Christ to us. We are grateful for the team at Vitas Healthcare who served us in such life-giving ways at the end of Steve's life, including Mitsy Kirkland, Tom Livengood and Marilyn Washburn, who were always a phone call away. We are also indebted to CaringBridge, an amazing website that enabled us to communicate with those we know and those we will never know. Thank you to InterVarsity Press: publisher, Bob Fryling, managing editor, Ben McCoy, and his team, and Cindy Bunch, our editor, who with lightning speed have created this book. The list goes on and on. We can only say thank you.

God did something amazing during Steve's last week. From the first night when we called our children to come, a little community including Bill and Peggy Scheu, Doug and Jean Taylor, Maggie, Fiona and Logan, Bobby and Charlene Gross, Tim and Saranell Hartman, Simeon, Elliana and Jeremiah, James B. and Renee Notkin and Marilyn Washburn gathered day and night in our sunroom, living room and kitchen to keep vigil with us. Food magically arrived while love was served up in Starbucks to-go cups, Revolution donuts and fried eggs. Listening ears and praying hearts, attentive to our needs as a family, created a deep awareness throughout that week of the Spirit's presence in our home, among these friends.

During Steve's last hour on earth, as Emilie, Chip, Drew, Thomas Daniel and I gathered around Steve's bed, these dear friends gathered on the back stairs outside our bedroom door—like the angels that seven-year-old Elliana Hartman said she saw going up and down our stairs several days earlier. As we read Scripture to Steve, they read Scripture and texted it to Chip's wife, Kristen, in Nashville and Thomas's wife and girls, Beth, Hannah and Miriam, in Austin. As we sang, they sang—sounding like an angel choir joining the heavenly choir who awaited Steve at the gates of heaven. As we prayed, they prayed. Together we accompanied Steve home to his rest with Jesus.

We could only go so far, but we caught a glimpse into the wonder and beauty of the place Jesus had prepared for Steve. We were a part of something so much bigger than us, part of the kingdom of God where saints and angels from all times and places ring God's throne singing, "Holy, holy, holy." It was a *thin place* where earth and heaven meet. Despite the incredible agony of those moments, we were convinced that "in life and in death, we belong to God." We know what it is to be lost in the mystery of wonder, love and praise—and overwhelming sadness. In our grieving and sorrow, we acknowledge God's goodness and faithfulness. This part of the journey is now over. Now the next chapter begins.

Notes

June 1

pp. 45-46 "When you speak to me": Parker Palmer, *A Hidden Wholeness* (San Francisco: Jossey-Bass, 2004), p. 117.

June 10

p. 50 c.c. cummings, "i thank You God for most this amazing," in *100 Selected Poems* (New York: Grove, 1954).

July 9

p. 60 "The burden of suffering": attributed to Julius Richter, quoted in L. B. Cowman, *Streams in the Desert* (1925; repr., Grand Rapids: Zondervan, 1997), p. 266.

August 7

pp. 71-72 "Where the ripple goes": Steve Moore, "The Ripple," May 2012. Used by permission.

August 16

p. 75 "Joy is the serious business": C. S. Lewis, *Letters to Malcolm: Chiefly on Prayer* (Orlando: Harcourt, 1964), p. 93.

November 5

p. 101 His powerful resignation speech: Robertson McQuilkin, "Robertson McQuilkin's Resignation Speech," YouTube video, 1:48, from McQuilkin's resignation from Columbia International University, March 1990, posted by "Trinity

Church Redlands, CA," February 10, 2014, www.youtube.com/watch?v=MqtG-XfxMC4.

p. 101 — and subsequent book (*A Promise Kept*): Robertson McQuilkin, *A Promise Kept: The Story of an Unforgettable Love* (Carol Stream, IL: Tyndale, 1998).

pp. 101-2 — "It's sundown, Lord": Robertson McQuilkin, "Let Me Get Home Before Dark," 1981. Used by permission.

November 26

p. 108 — "joy is the serious business of Heaven": C. S. Lewis, *Letters to Malcolm: Chiefly on Prayer* (Orlando: Harcourt, 1964), p. 93.

December 17

pp. 116-17 — "Is there grace enough to cover": Stephen Hayner, "Advent," November 18, 1990.

January 30

pp. 128-29 — "The Flying Rodleighs": Henri J. Nouwen, *Our Greatest Gift: A Meditation on Dying and Caring* (San Francisco: HarperSanFrancisco, 1995), p. 66.

January 31

pp. 130-31 — "My favorite unique memory": Steve Harrington, email to Presbyterian Pastors National Covenant Group, July 25, 2014.

February 18

p. 137 "Grieving is such strange sorrow!": unpublished poem by Ken Old. Used by permission of Patty West.

Epilogue

p. 140 "Joy is the serious business of Heaven": C. S. Lewis, *Letters to Malcolm: Chiefly on Prayer* (Orlando: Harcourt, 1964), p. 93.

Sidebar Contributors

Mary Anona Stoops	June 26
Linda Breeden	May 23
Linda Doll	October 20
Kevin Ford	January 30
W. Mark George	December 25
Priscilla Lasmarias Kelso	July 9
Sarah (Zimmerman) MacIntosh	November 26
Ed Ollie Jr.	December 17
John Ortberg	June 25
Stan Ott	September 3
Greta Reed	January 2
Alison Siewert	August 6
Tim Teusink	February 18
Martha Thompson Wagner	May 26
Andy Wade	September 24
Sue Westall	May 12